Lady Castaways

Lady Castaways

Joan Druett

LADY CASTAWAYS

AN OLD SALT PRESS BOOK, published by Old Salt Press, a Limited Liability Company registered in New Jersey, U.S.A.

For more information about our titles, go to
www.oldsaltpress.com

First published in 2015

© 2015 Joan Druett

ISBN 978-0-9941152-6-3 (eBook)

ISBN 978-0-9941152-7-0 (print edition)

Cover image © 2015 Ron Druett

Interior art © 2015 Ron Druett

Also by Joan Druett

Contents

ONE

The Nantucket Cook

Any woman who stepped aboard a ship that was bound to exotic Pacific destinations must have felt a fair number of qualms, shipwreck being one of the foremost. Death by drowning was dreaded by mariners of both sexes, but being cast away on a tropical island—where, as was popularly known, free love was practiced—held particularly dire implications for a decent lady. Cannibalism was another ghastly prospect. If shipwreck should indeed happen, the best she could hope for, perhaps, was that the island where she was cast up by the sea was uninhabited.

According to an old sea captain, Roland F. Coffin, this last is exactly what happened to one seafaring woman. His story started in the whaleboat where he was one of the oarsmen, at the moment when everyone realized that they'd got lost after being towed a long way off by a fighting whale. After thirty-six hours of sailing and rowing about in a fruitless quest for the sight of a sail, the six men were faint for lack of food and water, so the captain ordered his boat's crew to abandon the search and head for the distant islet that one of the seamen had glimpsed on the horizon.

It took all night to work up to the island, so they did not land until dawn. Too small to be charted, it seemed quite deserted, but at least it offered the chance of a drink of coconut milk, if not fresh water. Then one of the boys — a Nantucketer by the name of Tom Bunker — let out a yell that he had scented a spring, and when they followed his lead, they found a pool of beautiful clear water in among some rocks and trees. They drank their fill, then finally straightened to look around.

"Odd thing that there ain't no birds," said Tom Bunker thoughtfully. "Uninhabited islands always have thousands of birds" — and, while the others were digesting this strange statement, a solitary figure rushed out of the coconut palms, and then stopped dead, wavering back and forth in obvious uncertainty and disbelief.

"It's a native," said the captain. After waving to the others to keep back, he approached the figure in a friendly fashion, doing his utmost with gestures to demonstrate that he meant no harm, and finally the figure allowed the captain to come close. At which, to the seamen's surprise, both the captain and the native let out a yell of amazement, and the native began to caper about.

It was then that they found it was a tattered and weather-beaten American female — and a female from their home port of Nantucket, at that. "It ain't no dream; you are real," she cried, according to Coffin. "Thank God, I am saved!"

She was the wife of the captain of a whaleship that had foundered on the reef. After being washed ashore, she had found to her horror that she was the only survivor. Being a resourceful soul, though, she had managed remarkably well. She had scavenged the wreck for materials for a cabin, and then, having built it, she had settled down to wait for rescue. She had been waiting, in fact, for five years — but now, by the grace of God, she was saved!

"Well, as to that, ma'am," said the captain, and hemmed and hawed a bit — while of course, he said, they would do everything in their power to help her, whether she was saved or not was a matter of opinion, because they were in great need of being saved themselves. Not only had they mislaid their ship, but they were starving, it being a number of days since their last meal.

Though naturally disappointed, the castaway rallied fast. First, she took them to the little hut she had built, and then she told them to sit down outside and relax while she cooked them some breakfast. "Of course I didn't expect company," she said, so it would take a little while to get things together, but all they needed was to be patient.

And off she went into a grove of coconuts, where Coffin, to his mystification, saw her running back and forth with a lump of wood, hitting the ground every now and then. He, like the others, did not wonder about it very long, however. All six men were exhausted after their many hours of pulling at oars, and so they stretched out on the sand for a nap. And then, as Coffin reminisced, they woke up to "one of the finest smells of cooking I ever smelt."

Breakfast was stewing in a pot she had retrieved from the wreck five years before, and which was now steaming over a fire. "And if you don't say it's a good stew," she said, "then call me a bad cook." And then she served out the stew in coconut shell bowls, and it was brown and rich and smelling very savory indeed.

The men fell upon the food, Coffin reminiscing, "The woman looked on quite delighted for to see us eat, and a-fillin' each chap's dish as fast as it was empty." Finally, she couldn't persuade them to eat a scrap more. Then, as she took the coconut bowls away, she observed, "I bet you don't any of you know what you've been eatin'."

"Well, ma'am," prevaricated the skipper, and admitted

that he couldn't rightly guess, though, as he added, "it was a powerful good stew, and shows that you're a first-class cook, but that of course you would be, coming from Nantucket."

"Well," said she, "that there was a rat stew." The ship rats had survived the wreck and bred on the island, and because they had destroyed all the birds' nests on the island, she had been forced to live on those rats for all the five years she had been here.

Unfortunately for the men, they had to do the same. Being so resourceful, she gave them a varied menu, of "roast rat, broiled rat, fried rat, rat fricassee, and rat stew," but, as Coffin concluded, relief was general when their ship found them, and they sailed away, leaving the rats in full possession of the isle.

Western Sub-Antarctic

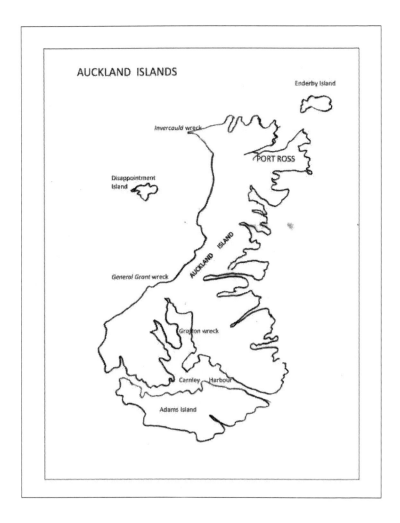

TWO

Mary Ann Jewell

It is interesting that Roland F. Coffin, the narrator of the Nantucket woman's story, did not name the heroine – out of tact, probably, because she wouldn't have had a chance of living it down if the gossip got around that she had lived on rats for five years, Nantucket being such a small community. It is unfortunate, though, that he did not go into any details of her castaway experience. What was her hut like, and how did she build it? And how did she manage to scavenge so much from the wreck?

A famous example of a man who did go into technical details was François Raynal, the mate and the supercargo of the sealing schooner *Grafton,* which was carried by a storm onto a reef at Auckland Island in the sub-Antarctic, at midnight on January 3, 1864. After struggling ashore, Raynal and the four other crew of the *Grafton* faced a daunting prospect. Icy, wet and storm-swept at all seasons of the year, Auckland Island is not just uninhabited, but almost impenetrable, the steep cliffs clothed with dense, tangled iron-hard shrubbery, and the levels at the top clothed in soggy tussock, and fissured with deep ravines. Probably worst of all for the marooned men was the oppressive silence, punctuated only by the thud and boom of surf, a constant reminder that they were almost three hundred miles away from the nearest inhabited land. Raynal, however, was unusually well suited to cope with the challenge. Over the past eleven years, he had lived rough on the Australian goldfields, and before that he had been an engineer and overseer on the island of Mauritius.

The *Grafton* castaways had quite a few blessings to count as they cowered in their makeshift, sodden tent the morning after the disaster. Raynal's hard-earned skill in living off the land was not the only thing on their side. They had matches, so could light a fire. The island was a seasonal breeding platform for sea lions, so it was possible — though at great risk — to club and kill the animals for meat and leather. There was abundant fresh water. The wreck of the schooner was accessible at low tide, being held high and fast on the reef. François Raynal had brought a rifle with him, with some ammunition. Crucially, their skipper, Captain Thomas Musgrave, was a decisive and capable leader, and the small band of five castaways had a strongly uniting sense of brotherhood.

The priority was to make a ramp for the ship's boat, as the dinghy was essential not just for exploring the bays and charting the coast, but for venturing out after game. Once the boat was safely beached, the next urgent matter was to find a site for a cabin. A terrace overlooking the wreck and the landing place that close to a fine spring of fresh water was chosen, and a good area of this scraped and leveled. Then the men measured out a rectangle, twenty-four feet long and sixteen feet wide. A four-foot-deep hole was dug at each corner of this, and masts from the wreck were planted as corner-posts, and wedged in with stones and packed dirt. The heads of these posts, seven feet from the ground, were notched to take crossbeams, which were also made from spars that had been salvaged from the wreck. Two more holes were dug in the middle of each of the shorter ends of the rectangle, to take two much taller poles, cut from the mainyard of the *Grafton*. The bowsprit was slung between these, forming the ridge-pole, and so the party had the skeleton of a roof.

Rafters had to be made from local timber, which was gnarled and twisted, and hard to cut, but they had both determination and an ax, which they sharpened with a grindstone fashioned from a ballast block. The roof was covered in with canvas, and then more poles from the wreck were salvaged for door posts and a lintel, leftover lengths being used to make the framework for a fireplace. This frame was filled in with flat stones cemented together with a mortar that Raynal made from crushed, burned seashells mixed with sand. Then a chimney was added, lined with plates of copper wrenched from the schooner's hull. Meantime, two men went out cutting the straightest branches they could find, to form the upright studs of the walls. The spaces between these were closed in with stripped branches laced together, and then the whole was thatched with tussock. Finally, a door was made and hung, and the floor was planked with timber torn from the decks of the schooner.

The job had taken thirty-one long, arduous days, but at last the five *Grafton* castaways had a refuge — a cabin that was staunch enough to keep them warm and alive for the many months it took to build a seaworthy boat. It stood for many years after that, but it was not long before it served to shelter another set of castaways — fourteen men and one woman, who were stranded just one year after the *Grafton* crew had saved themselves by crossing the roughest sea in the world to find help in New Zealand.

The American sailing ship *General Grant* departed from Melbourne, Australia, on May 4, 1866, with eighty-five souls on board — 25 crew and 58 passengers, many of them fresh from the goldfields of Victoria — and a hoard of gold stowed in with the mixed cargo in the holds. After skirting the south of Tasmania, the captain steered east. He was was sailing the Great Circle route to Cape Horn, flying on the prevailing westerly gales in latitude fifty. This was a popular choice in those days, as it offered a course that was unimpeded all the way to the southern tip of South America — unimpeded, that is, except for Auckland Island, which became notorious as the graveyard of ships that blundered onto its precipitous western cliffs in a fog, or a blinding snow squall, or in the dark.

It was ten-thirty at night when the lookout on the bow shouted a warning of land dead ahead. The *General Grant* had been running free all day, cutting through a very rough sea. The officer on deck yelled to the helmsman to put the wheel hard to port. The watch ran to the braces to bring the yards round, and the ship sheered off. But the land sighted had not been the western coast of Auckland Island, as calculated — instead it was an offshore islet named Disappointment Island. This meant that when the ship was brought back on her eastward course, she was steering straight into disaster. Streaming cliffs reared out of the night — grim, precipitous walls of granite that were known to seamen as the Jaws of Hell. It was impossible to steer off, however. The captain could do nothing to avoid impending catastrophe, and was forced to watch helplessly as the ship sagged closer and closer to the rocks. The wind had dropped to a dead calm, leaving the ship at the mercy of the strong landward swell.

A half-hour after midnight, the ship sailed not just onto the rocks, but into the cliff itself. She had been washed into a great cavern, which absorbed her bows and rigging in a cacophony of breaking spars. Everyone rushed into the cabins, to get out of the way of the collapsing yards and the rocks that had been dislodged from the roof of the cave. Once they were inside they cowered in a horde of trembling bodies, men trying to reassure women and women trying to comfort children, as they waited out the terrifying hours of utter, cave-bound blackness. It was impossible not to feel convinced that at every jerk and surge that the ship would sink and drown them all, despite the captain's constant reassurances. To make the ordeal even more nerve-wracking, the stump of the main mast banged repeatedly on the rock overhead as the tide rose and the swells rolled in. It was as if the granite roof was a hammer, driving the foot of the great mast down through the hull to smash a huge hole that would take her down to the bottom of the sea. Said one of the survivors, seaman Joseph Jewell, "such a night of horror I think was never experienced by human beings." To make the experience even more terrible, his young bride, Mary Ann, was with him.

It must have seemed it at times that the blackness would engulf them forever, but with dawn a gray light seeped into the cave. At once, urged on by the captain, the men set to clearing the wreckage from the three boats that were lashed bottom-up on the deck. A studdingsail boom was rigged with a block and whip, and the first boat was launched over the stern, which was projecting out of the cave. Then three men were inside her, carrying 250 fathoms of rope and a lump of iron for an anchor.

The plan was to run the boat out the full length of the line, then anchor her to the reef. This would make her a floating platform, so that the other boats could be hauled out hand-over-hand, once they were loaded with people. The surf was still high and the tide still rising, so the prospects were dangerous in the extreme, but it was the one scant hope of escape. A quick survey had been more than enough to confirm that it was impossible to scale the 600-foot cliff that overhung the cavern.

As the tide rose the mast thumped harder against the roof of the cave, a giant sound that reverberated over and over, as the rock walls threw back echoes. The main deck had slumped to sea level, and waves were washing over the stern. Nevertheless the first mate of the ship, Bart Brown, managed to launch the second boat. It dipped and surged with every swell, while he and the four other men inside her struggled to hold her still. Joseph Jewell pulled off his seaman's neckerchief, and tied it around Mary Ann's head. He wrote later that he did this to keep her hair out of her eyes, but it may have been to blindfold her, so she couldn't see the terrifying rocks and water below. He then lashed a rope about her waist, and lowered her overboard. She threshed, increasingly drenched by the flick of the waves as he dropped her further. Joseph was aiming for the wildly dipping boat, but missed every time. The boat kept filling with water with every wash-back of the waves, which meant that it surged and rocked with its constantly changing weight, while the men inside it frantically baled.

Finally, a burly goldminer by the name of James Tier staggered to his feet, reached up, and made a grab at Mary Ann's body. He managed to get a grip on her skirts, but when he hauled her up to the side of the boat they simply pulled up to her waist. Seeing that his wife was on the verge of slipping out of her dress and drowning, Joseph jumped overboard, sinking deep into icy salt water. Struggling upwards, he got hold of her and pushed — and at long last Mary Ann tumbled over the gunwale and into the boat, as wet, cold and battered as a hooked fish. Joseph then flopped into the bottom, and, seeing this, two more men jumped off the ship and managed to fling themselves over the side. Then the boat could hold no more.

By hauling on the rope, they brought up the boat to the side of the anchored one, and four men and Mary Ann were handed into it. That done, Joseph Jewell and the other seamen turned the boat back to pick up more people from the ship. When they were about a hundred yards off they saw the longboat float overboard with about forty people inside, but then, to Jewell's horror, the longboat filled with the wash-back from the stern, and turned turtle. And, with a dreadful wrenching and groaning of timbers, "the vessel sunk at the same time in 18 fathoms of water." The last they saw of the *General Grant* was the captain in the mizzen topmast crosstrees, calmly waving his handkerchief. Only three men were saved as they swam out from the capsized boat, while the cave echoed shrilly with the anguished screams of men, women and children who were struggling through their last minutes out of the reach of a helping hand, the surf being far too high to venture a boat inside.

Of the eighty-three souls who had sailed on the *General Grant,* just fifteen could now be counted — four passengers, and eleven crew. Of the nine women who had boarded the *General Grant,* Mary Ann was the only survivor. Fifteen children were amongst the names of the drowned. One of the surviving passengers, goldminer Nicholas Allen, must have been suffering an agony of conscience, as he had abandoned his wife and children when he followed Joseph Jewell and jumped overboard. According to stories told later, they had begged him not to leave them to drown, but he had been deaf to their pleas. Bart Brown, the first mate, had left his wife when he had launched the second boat. Now, hunched and gray, both men knew they would never see their wives again.

Grimly, the seamen turned the two boats into a rough sea and a hard gale with snow — the wind that could have saved them the night before had now risen. The waves flung high, and those who were not pulling oars had to bale all the time. First, they tried the shore of the mainland, but the cliffs defeated them. They then rowed to Disappointment Island, but with the wind and the waves against them, they were unable to land. To make their case even more wretched, most of the provisions they had managed to save were lost when one of the boats swamped. With what must have seemed the last of their strength, the men in the second boat reached the upturned craft, righted it, and baled it out, then saved her crew by throwing out a rope to where they were floundering in the icy sea.

That particular crisis finally over, they turned back for the mainland, slowly and painfully hauling north along the coastline and rounding the cape at the top, heading for a harbor where they believed they would find a castaway cache of provisions. Altogether, as Joseph Jewell remembered, "We were three days in the boats and wet through all the time and bitter cold." At long last they made Port Ross, a sheltered inlet in the north-east of Auckland Island, and were finally able to beach the boats and stretch their cramped legs. Mary Ann was the worst off, as she had had so little exercise in the boat. She limped slowly and badly, and it took months before she could walk normally again.

While she rested, the men spread out, looking for what they could find. In the search of the islands that had followed the highly publicized plight of the crew of the wrecked *Grafton,* the government of Victoria, Australia, was supposed to have left life-saving supplies somewhere in Port Ross. Right now, though, the *General Grant* castaways could find nothing except a bottle with a message saying that goats and rabbits had been released.

Realizing that they would have to save themselves, they turned to the few provisions they had brought with them in the boats. During the hours of lying in the lee of Disappointment Island, they had managed to club two nesting birds — a presage of the months that loomed ahead. Now, they opened one of their precious cans of soup with the fine idea of cooking the albatross flesh in the savory liquid — but to do any cooking they needed a fire. Someone — either James Tier or Bart Brown, according to which story was told later — had put six matches in his pocket before he left the ship, which promised a life-saving fire. But, to their horror, when the first match was struck, it merely crumbled. Despite elaborate care, the same happened with the next match, and the fourth and fifth. Then the party was down to the last one. Breath-held, they all watched with intensity as it was scratched over the paper — and to their intense relief it flared into life. They were very aware that the fire must never be let out, as they had no means of making another, but in the meantime they had warmth and a means of cooking food. Their only beds that night were wet branches that they pulled down from the trees, but at least their stomachs were reasonably full.

Next day, after a breakfast of limpets and mussels foraged from the beach, they sallied about the coast in the boats, and found a hut that had been built by one of the castaways of the past — probably by one of the few survivors of the wreck of the Scottish square-rigger *Invercauld*, which had crashed and sunk in the depths off the northwest of the island in May 1864. The little shack had collapsed and the roof had fallen to the ground, but they were able to reassemble it, after a fashion, and so they had a kind of shelter — a very cramped shelter for so many, but much better than they had had the night before. And so they began to establish themselves on this uninhabited island, embarking on a grim routine of searching the coasts and inland tussock and bush for signs of castaway depots, looking for the goats, rabbits and pigs that the message in the bottle had promised, and keeping body and soul together by clubbing seals and birds. It was a diet that gave them all severe diarrhea, but at least it kept them alive.

They also dug up roots of the local mega-herb, *Stilbocarpa polaris,* a plant with immense furled leaves that the *Grafton* castaways called "saccary," and which could be stewed and fried as a substitute for potato. While coarse and unpalatable, it provided much of the carbohydrate and some of the vitamins that their bodies were craving. Joseph Jewell also recorded eating stinging nettle leaves, though he did not mention whether they were stewed or eaten as a salad. This should have helped prevent scurvy, but before long all of them were tormented with gross swelling in their legs.

Strange stories are told of those early months, whispers that have been handed down by the descendants of the survivors. Everyone was in a terribly debilitated state, but with one woman existing among so many men, sexual tensions were bound to arise. According to gossip, one of the passengers, Patrick Caughey, "at times showed an alarming interest in Mrs. Jewell." When a seaman, Billy Scott, was heard to make an insulting remark to her, James Tier beat him up — he smashed Scott "to the ground with a powerful punch to the head." According to another story, Mary Ann was elected "governess of the island" to help keep order. Those who behaved badly were to be judged by the rest, with the threat of banishment to one of the offshore islets if found guilty. If the story is true, then the evil prospect of exile from the group was an efficient deterrent, because the punishment was never carried out.

There were also whispers of cannibalism. There was already a tradition of this on the island. Back in May 1864, at the same time that the *Grafton* castaways were settling into their comfortable cabin in the south, the Scottish square-rigger *Invercauld* had crashed into northwestern cliffs, not many miles from the future grave of the *General Grant,* spilling her entire crew into an icy night. Of these, only nineteen had struggled ashore. From then on, their existence had been the stuff of nightmare. Their captain descended into a kind of numb madness, so exerted no leadership whatsoever, and the advice of the only seaman who had been on the goldfields and knew how to build a hut and forage for food was ignored, as he had no status, not being an officer. Within weeks, most of the *Invercauld* castaways died of starvation — but not before at least one had gnawed on the dead body of a companion, and others had attacked one of their number with the intention of killing him for food.

Did anything like this happen with the *General Grant* group? Months after his rescue, Billy Sanguilly, the youngest of the survivors, intimated that he had gone in fear of his life at the start of the ordeal. He had overheard plans for casting lots for a victim when the food ran out — or so he claimed. The man who drew the shortest straw would be given a head start before being chased down and killed. According to other whispers, this actually happened — except that the man who was being chased fell over a cliff and drowned while running from his murderous pursuers, instead of being eaten. Ironically, while blundering panic-stricken through the bush, he disturbed a herd of wild pigs.

Where the truth lies is impossible to tell, as none of the castaways published a book about their ordeal. This was most unusual, in an age where there was a great public appetite for tales of true-life adventures in remote, exotic spots. James Tier kept a diary scratched on dried seal skin, but nothing was done to turn it into a book. Was this because there was much that should be left unsaid?

It is a fact that the *General Grant* castaways did find pigs and rabbits, just as the message in the bottle promised. Catching the hogs was not an easy job, but then Tier, having had a brainwave, strung a stout hook onto a line, and used this to "fish" for pigs, snagging them as they browsed. The rabbits, it seems, were trapped. Joseph Jewell complained later that the meat was dry, probably because they did not have anything tasty to add to the stews. Having an alternative to sea lion meat was a great improvement to their bill of fare, however.

There was also a leadership issue. James Tier, being big, burly, and with years of experience of living off the land in the Australian goldfields and in New Zealand bush, was the logical overseer. Bart Brown, on the other hand, was the leader in name, as he had been the first mate of the *General Grant*. This appears to have led to some conflict between the two, but it did not prove as serious as it could have been, as Brown was a man who was restless by nature. He was often away exploring, with seamen as companions, leaving Tier in charge of the camp.

Two of these absences were on lengthy boat expeditions. While the first was unsuccessful, Bart and his men returning seven days later on the point of death from dysentery, the second penetrated Carnley Harbour, in the south of the island. This led to a significant discovery. On July 11, 1866, while exploring the great inlets, Brown located the large and sturdy cabin that the *Grafton* crew had built. Disappointingly, while the thatched house was still sound, there was no cache of provisions inside, but just another bottle with the same infuriating message about the pigs, goats and rabbits. Bart decided to move there, however, and six men volunteered to live there with him. Not only did this mean that the hut at Port Ross was less crowded, but it left Tier in complete charge of that camp, while Bart Brown was in control of the Carnley Harbour group. Additionally, it removed the two men who had been lasciviously eyeing Mary Ann Jewell from the temptation to bother her further. More practically still, it also doubled the company's chances of sighting a ship.

For those who remained at Port Ross there was another discovery — the ruins of a whaling station that had been established in one of the inlets, back in 1849. Called Hardwicke, the station had been the brainchild of a London oil and ship merchant, Charles Enderby. In its heyday, the village of whalemen and their families, plus carpenters, administrators and a surgeon, had consisted of eighteen pre-cut cottages, a government house, a barracks and a jail, and a number of workshops. It was not to last for long, however. The whaling had proved as bad as the problem with law and order — the colonists, after one horrified look at their new surroundings, had taken to the bottle, distilling their own spirits when liquor was banned, which had led to the need for a jail. In 1852 the project was abandoned, and the colonists departed after dismantling most of the buildings.

Whatever had been left had fallen down, so that when the *General Grant* castaways stumbled over the settlement, only grassed-over foundations remained. Naturally, they fossicked for anything useful, turning over some flint for making fire, and some pieces of sheet iron that served for frying slabs of meat, as an alternative to cooking stew in soup tins. The best find was a little cast iron oven, stumbled over during yet another wide search of Port Ross for anything left by the government for castaways. This proved most useful for boiling salt water to extract salt, so they could attempt to preserve seal meat for the lean months ahead. They also found a few potatoes, but instead of eating them they planted them, again with the future in mind. In the same spirit, they were keeping some of the pigs they captured alive, to form a breeding stock. For this they needed a boar, and when they successfully snared a young one, they named him Roger, and made him the camp's pet, while the chief sow was called Nellie.

Clothes had turned into rags in the rough conditions, boots in particular. James Tier ground needles from albatross bones, and used fiber from flax (a plant carried to Auckland Island by a Maori party in the 1840s) as cobbling thread, and made them all moccasins. With much trial and error, they found out how to skim thin, flexible sheets from cured sea lion hides, and Mary Ann Jewell cut and sewed these to make trousers and tunics for them all. When fur seals were caught their hides were eagerly cured, as the pelts were so much softer. Skins from fur seals were also turned into sleeping bags, while rabbit fur was made into mufflers. Cleanliness was another problem, as they were all very dirty and lice-ridden. Washing down with lye that they had made by boiling wood ashes in water was their only recourse, as no one thought of mixing the lye with seal oil, then boiling it up into soap — but on the whole they were quite comfortable, particularly when compared to their wretched condition when they had first arrived.

On October 6, 1866, when the *General Grant* castaways had been on the island for almost five months, a ship was sighted by the party in the north. As Joseph Jewell wrote, "you can imagine our joy" — and, for a wonder, the weather was fine, the sea quiet and calm. Leaving Mary Ann to tend signal fires, four of the men set out in a boat, and "got within two miles of her then the wind freshened and she passed on without taking any notice of us in the boat or the signal fires on shore and I am sure they must have seen the smoke." It was dark by the time the four men, weary, heartsick and disappointed, got back to the camp. Mary Ann was almost as badly off, as she had torn her clothes in the struggle to get the wood to keep the fires fed.

In December, Bart Brown arrived from Carnley Harbour with the news that he had decided to take a boat to New Zealand. He had no compass or charts, no nautical instruments at all, but the bad news of the passing ship would have only reinforced his determination to try the terrible voyage. The whole party helped, covering the boat with sea lion leather to make the interior more watertight, blowing up sea lion bladders and drying them for holding drinking water, and stocking the boat with all the food they could spare, along with a goat and two kids.

On January 22, 1867, Mary Ann, with the rest of the castaways, watched from the beach as the boat rowed off with a crew of four brave and desperate men. The three seamen with Bart Brown were Billy Scott, Peter Morrison and Peter McNevin. Slowly, the boat bobbed away, and then the seal skin sail was raised and the boat was gone — "never to be heard of again in this world," wrote Mary Ann's husband, Joseph Jewell, "but I hope to meet them again in heaven."

Not long after the boat had gone, they found an ax — a great blessing, as they could now cut firewood. It also meant that they could build log huts, which they did on Enderby Island, just north of the camp in Port Ross. That this was a better place for signaling ships was the reason Jewell gave for the other men moving there, but he gave no reason for staying behind with Mary Ann, taking sole charge of the Port Ross camp. If it was also a good idea to remove the men from the feminine temptation of his wife, it was undoubtedly better not mentioned.

One man stayed with them — sixty-two-year-old Scot David McLelland, who was an invalid. He had cut his hand on a sharp edge of copper when working with a group that was trying to scavenge materials off the wreck of the *Grafton* in Carnley Harbour, and the cut had refused to heal. Despite Mary Ann's nursing, his condition gradually deteriorated, and on November 3, 1867, he passed away, probably from blood poisoning. "To see the ten that was left standing round his new dug grave was sad indeed," wrote Joseph Jewell. It was nine months since Bart Brown and his three companions had vanished into the stormy seas, and sixteen months since their ship had wrecked.

Not long afterward, on November 19, another ship was sighted — in a fog that was so dense that the lookout failed to see their signal fires. But, just two days after that, on November 21, 1867, the New Zealand whaling brig *Amherst* put into the harbor, "and rescued us from our miserable condition and words cannot express the joy we felt when we arrived on the vessels deck; the Capt. and crew did everything they could for us and I think they were as glad at finding us as we were at seeing them."

The *Amherst* was on a sealing voyage, so could not leave until the season was over, but finally, on January 6, 1868, the castaways "bid goodbye to the Auckland Islands and in four days after we arrived at Bluff Harbour in Southland New Zealand and the kindness we received at the hands of the inhabitants on the Bluff and Invercargill will never be forgotten by us; they soon has us out of our sal skin clothes and supplied us with everything of the best."

Mary Ann Jewell was welcomed into the house of the port superintendent, where his wife fussed over her, and gave her clothes to replace her seal-skin tunic and trousers. So Mary Ann was dressed in a feminine gown when she met the newspaper reporters and testified in the court inquiry that followed. She had little to say to the Board, simply that she had paid her own passage, but had been shown how to sign articles as a stewardess, this being a legal requirement, as her husband was one of the seamen of the crew. She had not actually worked at the job, however — "No person on board acted as stewardess," she insisted.

While it seems that Mary Ann never learned how to read and write, she became a great deal more vocal after she and Joseph were settled in the town of Trafalgar, Victoria, Australia. Joseph was given the busy and important job of station-master, and Mary Ann made her own contribution to the depleted family finances — but not by sewing and nursing, as she had done on the island.

Instead, by taking advantage in the intense public interest in her castaway ordeal, she gave well-attended public lectures, earning as much as six hundred pounds a time. To add to the drama of what she was saying, she wore the seal skin suit she had made on the island. It was a major reason for the talks being so popular. Unfortunately, though, no one ever wrote down what she said.

Wreck of the American ship *General Grant,* from *Harper's Weekly*, May 16, 1868.

THREE

Emily Wooldridge

Another Englishwoman who went through an icy cold castaway ordeal in the sub-Antarctic was twenty-nine-year-old Emily Wooldridge. Like Mary Ann Jewell, Emily Wooldridge simply expected to pass a long voyage as happily and comfortably as she could. Instead — also like Mary Ann Jewell — she was headed for disaster and privation. Unlike Mary Ann, though, Emily was literate enough to leave a written description of her experience.

The ship, called *Maid of Athens,* was a very small brig, being registered at just 230 tons. Yet, despite her miniature dimensions, she was bound right across the world, to the Pacific coast of South America, with a mixed cargo that included camphor. It was a first command for Emily's husband, Richard Gurney Wooldridge, and as she had no children to hold her to the land, she was able to keep him company, which pleased her greatly. And, having traveled often as a passenger, she did not expect anything terrible to happen, even though the route included a doubling of dreaded Cape Horn.

"We left the London Docks the end of November, 1869, with twelve souls on board," she wrote, and then went on to describe the captain's private quarters. There were easy chairs in the day cabin, and watercolors on the walls, while in the sleeping cabin there was a full-sized iron bedstead, with trunks of clothes underneath; a chest of drawers with a mirror, a sofa with lockers underneath and a horsehair cushion on top; a washstand, and bookshelves. "I flattered myself I was as comfortable as any lady on the land."

The voyage began well. Emily amused herself with wool embroidery, reading, watching the waves break, and talking with her husband and his mate, who was the sturdy and reliable John Yates. On Sundays the cabin boy would practice his reading and writing lessons by reading from the Bible and the whole ship's company would pray. They even had visitors at sea. A whaleship lay nearby during a calm, and the captain came on board with four of his crew — "he told us he had come to *gam*, which means to visit another ship at sea." Captain Wooldridge gave him some potatoes and onions and a ham, and he gave them "a splendid harpoon out of his boat." Emily thought she might enjoy being rowed about the ship in the visitor's whaleboat, but when the time came she was too frightened to get down into it — "the boat looked so small I did not like to trust myself in it."

So all went sunnily, the brig escaping battering by storms until January 26, 1870, when they were off the River Plate, abreast of Montevideo. At noon, just as the captain was taking a sight of the sun, a squall blew up and a huge wave descended upon them, breaking the skylight — "the ship was on her beam ends. I was sent against the bulkhead deluged and gasping ... Then came the dreadful cry from on deck, *Two men overboard!*" The mate, John Yates, and the cabin boy, John Williams, had been washed into the tempest-torn sea.

Emily Wooldridge did something odd — she seized her

scissors and cut off her long skirts. It was a presage of the instincts that were to save her later. Freed of the encumbrance, she rushed up to deck, to see that the boy was struggling to reach one of the buoys that had been thrown overboard, and that there was no sign of John Yates. The ship cast back and forth, but while the boy was saved, Yates was never glimpsed again.

This was a double tragedy for the ship and the captain. Yates had been a thorough seaman who had the respect and obedience of men who otherwise would have shirked their work. Without him, there was no one who could be trusted to take charge of the deck. The atmosphere as the brig sailed on toward Cape Horn was doleful and grim, with a captain who became exhausted from constantly keeping the watch.

On February 16, 1870, the coast of Patagonia was raised, and then the Atlantic end of the Straits of Magellan, which was one of the tortuous seaways to the Pacific Ocean. Captain Wooldridge kept going south, however. He was steering for the Straits of La Maire, at the lowest tip of South America, to get to the Pacific Ocean by sailing between Staten Island and Tierra del Fuego and passing Cape Horn.

But, having no mate to help con the ship, he decided to stand off until daylight instead of risking the passage in the dark. Accordingly, when two bells was struck for nine in the evening, the brig was going nowhere, simply rolling heavily under short sail. Captain Wooldridge was lying on the sofa, trying to rest, when he was shocked awake by a man shouting out, "On deck quick, sir!"

With a thump of boots he left the cabin, but was quickly back down the companionway, crying out for a lantern. Emily jumped up, and when she went into the sleeping cabin to fetch the lantern that was hanging there, she saw to her horror that the bulkhead behind the bed was oozing thick smoke. "I seized my stockings," she wrote, and then two boots — "in stooping for which I saw the ship's matches under my bed. I caught them up." Running up the stairs to deck, she put them into someone's hands, then down she went again to dress. Frantically, as she grabbed petticoats, she wondered what to save. "The ship's papers caught my eye in their tin box, only it was too full to shut. Out of my cabin again, saw a piece of string tying a chair to the door handle, took it off, bound the box and sent it on deck."

Then she pulled some clothes over the petticoats, still without taking off her nightgown. In her confusion she was choosing at random — a thin woolen jacket over her nightdress and the petticoats, then her dressing-gown, over that a shawl, and a covering for her head. At the same time the steward, who was a quick-witted and reliable man by the name of George Allen, was collecting provisions — bags of biscuits, tins of meat, a ham, a cheese, a half-full bag of flour, and knives, forks and spoons — "but in the midst of our bustle came the dreadful cry, *Get the boats ready!*"

Emily ran up the stairs through the billowing smoke, pursued by her little dog. Three steps up, the little dog died, either of fright or suffocation. There was no time for grief — glimpsing a rug, Emily called out to the steward to collect it. Then she was on deck, out in the dark and the panicked commotion. Seeing the boxes of matches she had sent up just minutes before lying neglected by the wheel, she put two of them in her pockets, and gave more to the helmsman, who was struggling to keep the burning vessel on course. This was for Staten Island, Captain Wooldridge's intention being to run the *Maid of Athens* up on the beach, and save as much cargo as he could.

Men were throwing buckets of water down the after hatchway, but it was to no avail. The camphor in the hold was smoldering hard, sending up gusts of acrid smoke. Unable to bear it any longer, the men shut the hatch, but the flames were coming up through the deck, flaring higher and hotter with every passing moment. Emily slumped to a perch on the poop deck, huddled under the rug, watching the men's struggle to contain the fire, and contemplating a terrifying future. She heard her husband give the order to shut the doors to the companionway as the smoke made the air unbreathable, but before anyone could obey the steward made a last dive down the stairs. The gallant fellow came back with his eyes streaming, carrying the sextant, a compass, and a chart. These went into the slung longboat, along with the provisions and everything else that had been saved.

A grudging daylight appeared on the horizon, to reveal a gray, turbulent sea and bleak mountains covered with snow. The brig rolled heavily, and the longboat knocked against her side. Thinking his wife would be more sheltered there, Captain Wooldridge told Emily to go forward to the galley, but as she walked over the deck planks she was shocked to find how hot they were. The men were equally shocked — to see how thinly she was clad. The steward made another dash down the stairs, to grope for more clothing, while the others opened the cabin skylight and let down a dangling hook, which they swung around, managing to snag blankets and sheets. Then the doors and skylight were hastily slammed shut. It was time to abandon ship.

"Feb. 16, 1870, the *Maid of Athens* on fire, Captain, wife and eight men running for Staten Island," wrote Captain Wooldridge on a scrap of paper, adding, "For God's sake come and help us." Then, after they had all had a bracing tot of gin mixed with water, to wash down the last of the steward's soft bread, he put the message in the empty gin bottle, shoved in the glass stopper, and threw the bottle overboard. "Where is that bottle now, I wonder?" wrote Emily later. As far as she knew, it was never found.

The longboat was ready to put down on the water, but still they waited. Emily was still in the galley, and the men were at various lookouts in the rigging and on the firmest parts of the burning deck, peering through the smoke for the hoped-for gradually sloping beach. The sun had come out, and the warmth it brought had added to the courage the gin had given them. More hopeful still was the sight of a cove with a rim of sand. Inside the bay, the water was smoother, and the *Maid of Athens* sailed steadily onward, until brought up as the hull grounded with a series of bumps. "We only struck three times, and then she heeled over slightly," wrote Emily; "the sea broke with great force over her and caused her to lurch over a little more."

Instinctive as ever in the moment of crisis, Emily snatched all the saucepans and frypans off the walls of the galley and threw them in the direction of the boat, following up with the big boiler, which she rolled along the deck to the rail. She ran back for the men's clothing that had been hung over the stove to dry, and then it was time to go over the side. Emily was lifted and put down into the hanging boat, just a hailstorm came up. The captain and one of the seamen, George Hayward, worked the boat falls from the deck — "the instant we touched the water, a tremendous sea came over us." The boat only narrowly escaped being swamped, and after that wave after wave deluged Emily as first Hayward and then the captain jumped down into the thwarts. Then they were off. Within seconds the surf rushed them up the beach, and within instants the men were heaving Emily, weighted down with her drenched clothes, onto the shore.

Everything was wet, including the boxes of matches Emily had stowed in her pocket. However the helmsman had put the ones she had given him into a tin tobacco box, so they were dry. Even more providentially, Captain Richard Wooldridge had past experience of living off the land in the goldfields of Australia, so that like many a seasoned bushman he knew how to make a shelter, and understood the priority of finding good fresh water. Seizing an ax, he hacked a way through the scrub that hemmed in the beach, following the sound of a running stream.

A small terrace spread out from the foot of a small cascade, and there he lit a fire in a nook for him and Emily. Another fire was made for the men, and shivering in another downpour, they huddled around it in their oilskins. Once, when Emily looked up, it was to see another fire at sea — the blaze that was destroying her husband's ship. She saw it flare up as it consumed what was left of the *Maid of Athens*. Then, with a double crash, the masts toppled down.

Next morning, Emily and the steward made an inventory of what they had managed to salvage, while the captain and men went down to the beach to see what might have been washed up. She listed two rugs, two pillows, a small box, a ruined chronometer, a sextant, telescope, two charts, one compass, two buckets, and some knives, along with two small saucepans and two frying pans. These were the only cooking utensils that had not been washed out of the boat and lost, though the big boiler had floated to the beach on its own. The bags of ship's biscuit had been soaked by the sea, so Emily and the steward rinsed off as much salt as they could with fresh water, and then set them by the fire to dry. Captain Wooldridge arrived from the beach with planks to make a bed, and finally Emily found a pencil and an account book, so was able to write down her list, and begin a diary.

Over the next few days the men risked death by going out to the smoldering wreck and fossicking for what they could find — tobacco, a small keg of rum, smoke-polluted rice, and water-damaged tea. There were bales of calico from the cargo, too, along with a few bags of potatoes. Meantime Captain Wooldridge, drawing on his experiences in the Australian outback, set to building a hut. Two straight, suitably placed trees were found, and trimmed down to forks, then a pole set into the forks to span the space between them and act as a roof-ridge. The ends of forked stakes were driven into the ground to make four sides that were somewhat lower than the ridge-pole, then braced along the top with more poles from the wreck. After that, three of the sides were thatched with saplings. Once calico had been stretched and stitched over the whole, they had a rudimentary dwelling, "one end being open for the door." Emily's bed was taken down and reassembled inside, "and we had a bed and a house!"

With every hazardous expedition to the foul-smelling, blackened remains of the brig their store of provisions was increasing. A cask of portable soup was retrieved, along with another cask of salted meat, cans of pickles and mustard, and bottles of assorted oils — cod-liver oil and castor oil, but no cooking oil. The cargo was drifting on shore in greater abundance as the hull broke up — bizarrely, one morning the beach was strewn with baby feeding bottles. These proved surprisingly useful, being handy as candle-holders. Managing to hoist out the galley stove and get it up the beach merited another celebration, though it never got up the hill to the camp.

When it was obvious that the fire was completely out Emily was brave enough to go out to the wreck herself. Her sleeping cabin was still recognizable, though the iron bedstead had warped completely out of shape, as had her portable bath. She managed to retrieve some spoons and forks, and a galvanized tin wash-bowl — "these I carried up to the camp." She and her husband even had seats — Emily asked one of the men to bring a bucket "up to my tent," and after a piece of wood was put across the top it served as her chair, while the captain sat on a tin that had held preserved potatoes. As planks were rescued, they were requisitioned to make a floor for their hut, meaning that Emily no longer had to live on top of mud.

So, within a remarkably short time, Emily and her husband were living not just under cover, but in reasonable comfort. The problem was that the men were not. Shipboard life was by no means democratic — the captain and his wife had the privileged after quarters, while the men lived in the crowded squalor of the forecastle. The captain and his wife had a steward and a cabin boy, and ate at a table, while the men sat on their sea chests in the forecastle to eat whatever had been dished out by the ship's cook, from tin plates in their laps. Like many a castaway captain, Richard Wooldridge saw no reason to change this social setup after his ship was wrecked — and neither did his wife. Accordingly, the house the captain had built (with the help of his men) was reserved for himself and Emily, the men being advised to build their own accommodation. This they did, but not even on the same site as the captain's cabin. Instead, they set up a calico shack by the waterfall, at their first resting place.

For some time the men did not seem to resent this — they, too, had taken the undemocratic state of affairs on board ship for granted. The steward still acted as the captain's servant, and so did the cabin boy. When Oates, one of the foremast men, noticed that Emily's boots were falling apart, he found another pair for her. They were men's big sea-boots, but she was "only too grateful to accept them." She lashed them onto her feet so they would not keeping falling off, and quickly learned how to stumble around. When a cask of salt beef was retrieved from the wreck, it was brought up to the captain's cabin as a matter of course. The ship's bell, retrieved from the quarter deck of the wreck, was set up outside his shack, so that Emily could summon the cabin boy whenever she wanted something done. Significantly, when Emily decided that the two huts should be given names, the one where she and the captain lived was called the Mount, while the men's calico tent was simply the Encampment.

Emily thought she was doing her best. She assisted by picking oakum as the men caulked the two boats, and helped the steward dry the salvaged flour. Then she baked bread to provision those boats for the escape they planned to make, hoping to reach the Falkland Islands, where there was a decent town at Port Stanley. She assisted her husband with the careful rationing out of provisions each day, so that the men got the same as she did. However, trouble was brewing.

One day, while the men were cutting spars from the wreck to make masts for the boats, Hayward and another seaman named Sargent had stayed on the beach, and were cutting a sail. Captain Wooldridge walked up to the sailmakers, took a glance at their work, told them they were cutting it wrong — and Sargent pulled a knife on him. The seaman was easily knocked down, and immediately began to blubber his apologies. However, it was a warning of the mood in the Encampment. Two days later, Emily missed the bottle of gin, reserved for medicinal purposes, that had been hidden under her pillow. And then, the day after that, more spirits were stolen from the Mount, while Emily and her husband were scavenging on the beach.

Considering their limited resources, and the damage that drunken men could do, this was considered equivalent to mutiny. Captain Wooldridge held a prayer meeting, where the men obediently sang hymns, and then he lectured them about the missing liquor. Nonetheless, despite Emily's vigilance, more liquor was stolen a week later. Then, as the party began to live almost entirely off the land, reserving the last of their provisions for the passage to the Falklands, the men came to the Mount in a rebellious group, muttering among themselves. Stepping forward, their spokesman demanded more bread. It was obvious that it wasn't just bread they wanted, so after sending them packing the captain bottled the remainder of the grog, went up into the woods, and buried it there. Frustratingly, just a few days later, when he was very ill and would have benefited from some brandy, he could not remember where he had stashed the liquor.

On March 8, the men launched the longboat with a significant list of goods inside — calico for a tent, enough provisions for four days, a bucket and saucepan, knives, and the ax. And then they sailed past the wreck and out of the bay. Only a half-witted seaman named Fielding and John the cabin boy were left behind. Obviously, Emily was alarmed, but as it turned out, the men had merely moved along to another beach. Two of them — Harris and the troublesome Sargent — returned that night to report that they had landed in another bay, a much better one for making the longboat seaworthy, as the beach was smoother, and the water more calm. The others, they said, had made a fire, and were starting on the construction of a calico shack — which was lucky, as when Harris and Sargent returned to the Encampment for the night, they accidentally set the old shack on fire.

Over the next few days the seamen trekked back and forth, rebuilding the Encampment and working on their new cabin in the other location, collecting planks and caulking material for the longboat, but at the same time demanding more provisions. When the captain gave them only enough for a day or so at a time, to make sure they kept on coming back, they stole the bread that had been saved for the passage to the Falklands.

Captain Wooldridge could not do much about it for some time, as he was too feeble to make the long walk to the seamen's bay, but at last he had recovered enough to set out on the trek. He returned the next day in a disgusted mood, telling Emily that no work had been done on the longboat, despite all the material he had sent over. Instead, the men were lying about in their new shack, grumbling about being hungry, because they had used up the whole day's ration at breakfast, and had nothing left for dinner or tea.

Probably because of this — but also because of the temptation of the liquor — the thefts continued. In desperation Wooldridge enlarged the Mount, with the ready cooperation of the steward. In effect, they built a whole new house around the old building, which now took up just a corner, and served as his and Emily's bedroom. Captain Wooldridge's idea was that the provisions could be kept in the rest of the new building, close to their sleeping quarters, and under the equivalent of lock and key. All their efforts proved useless. The morning after the new house was finished, Emily woke up to see drippings of molasses on the floor outside the bedroom, and when she followed the trail she found that rice and flour were missing. The men had crept in during the night — with sacking over their boots, or so she theorized — and removed the food without making a sound.

An even greater disappointment lay ahead. On March 19, while Captain Wooldridge and the steward were reinforcing the roof of the new house, Emily heard the cabin boy scream, "Sail ahoy! Ship ahoy!" When she jumped up, it was to see a ship close by. "Oh! Richard, a ship!" she cried, and began to run. Grabbing up matches and a lump of camphor, the captain and the steward raced after her down to the beach. Driftwood was scrabbled into a pile, and with trembling hands the steward struck a match. Finally the fire was burning, sending out billows of smoke, while the men tried to launch the small boat. The surf foiled them, upsetting them at once. Luckily, it was in shallow water, so they scrambled up, emptied it out, and set to launching it again. But Emily called out to them to save their strength. The ship was steering away.

The ship was so close that Emily could hear the yards go round. "She was painted black," she wrote, "and I could see people moving about the deck." Those people must have seen the fire, and the white sail of the boat, but still they sailed away. "Doubtless," she bitterly added, "they will meet with their reward."

Next day Emily was alone on the beach, as the captain had taken the small boat to the other camp, with more materials for the strengthening of the longboat. Sargent and Lawson arrived from the other camp, coming on the overland track. Marching right up to Emily, Sargent angrily demanded to know why the captain had not sailed the small boat out to the ship. Instead of ignoring him, Emily tried to explain, which made matters worse. She had to be rescued by the steward, who ran up, roughly pulled the men aside, and remonstrated with them.

Half-hysterical with shock, afraid that the men would openly raid the provisions, Emily hurried back to the Mount. It was a long time before her husband returned, and then her relief was short-lived, as Captain Wooldridge was suffering from a recurrence of his fever, and could only limp to bed. Next day he was almost crippled, but determinedly got up. The longboat was about ready, he told her, and despite his sick state he was determined that they should sail for the Falklands without delay. Two more ships had been sighted that day: it was obviously the season for the passage through the Straits of Le Maire, and if they did not go soon, the opportunity of being intercepted by a passing vessel would pass.

Harris, Lawson and Sargent, the three seamen who had made the most trouble, now mutinied openly, by flatly refusing to go in the longboat. For Emily and Captain Wooldridge, along with the more level-headed members of the crew, this was more of a relief than a worry. The small boat could be left for the pig-headed trio. If the three men saw a ship go by, they could sail out , and see if they could do better than the captain and the steward at seizing the lookout's attention. And they were not being abandoned to an endless castaway ordeal, as Wooldridge, being a conscientious master, would make coming back for them his first priority after getting safely to Port Stanley.

Accordingly, seven were to try the hazardous passage — the captain, Emily, the cabin boy, the steward, and three seamen, Hayward, Oates, and Fielding. Emily filled a cask with boiled tea that was sweetened with molasses, and packed matches, the compass, a pencil and notepaper in her small handbag. These, with a rug and blanket, and the captain's greatcoat, were put into the small boat, to be taken around to where the longboat was waiting at the other bay.

The small boat was launched, and then held still while two of the men carried her through the surf and put her into it. To Emily's discomfiture, that was the moment that she found she was more frightened of the surf than she was of the passage to the Falklands. Tensely, she watched the men as they held the boat and studied the waves, while she "sat perfectly still, holding my breath with fear."

After waiting for two or three seas to break, they all sprang inside and took up their oars, and with hearty hauling and a surge or two they were through the surf and rowing smoothly, much to Emily's relief. It was evening, and the light was growing dim as the stars came out, so she had a new view of the "frowning mountains" that rimmed the horizon behind their old camp.

Then they were in the new bay, where the longboat was floating at anchor. After so much time, the craft looked much bigger than remembered — "looking to my eyes like a yacht." Another relief was that the men greeted her politely, one taking her hand and assisting her up to the great blazing fire they had set. Planks had been laid to make a path, and when she arrived at the tent it was to find that it had been divided up with hanging sacks, so that she could have some privacy. That, with the salt pork that the steward fried up for tea, was immensely comforting.

Next day was Sunday, March 26, 1870. The longboat was launched, and four of the men pulled her slowly to the head of the bay, where they took the breeze, and hoisted the sail. "And so," wrote Emily, "we began our voyage."

The words were premature. Once they were fully out to sea, it was obvious that they would not survive many hours in the boat. The bulwarks were not high enough to shelter them from the icy spray, or to stop the craft filling with water and swamping. The only remedy was to go back to the bay, and raise the sides with a canvas screen to keep off the spray. And so, miserably wet, battered and seasick, they returned to the bay from whence they had come.

Strangely, the three men they had left behind were nowhere to be seen. When someone was sent to look for them, it transpired that the instant the longboat had been well away they had grabbed the opportunity to settle in what they considered the luxurious cabin at the Mount. Plenty of food had been left in their tent, however, so the party ate well, and the bulwarks were fixed the next day. And, the day after that, another attempt was made to leave the island. Once more, as Emily wrote, "we rowed out of the Bay, and when we felt the breeze, hoisted our sail and commenced our voyage." This time, they were successful. At last they were embarked on their passage to the Falklands.

The ordeal began almost immediately. Within hours they were passing ships that were going the opposite way, and which never bothered to alter their course to investigate the battered little craft. Then the sea was empty as before, rimmed with distant icy mountains, while the longboat surged and sank giddily. A cubby hole with a canvas drawn over the front had been made in the bows for Emily, and there she crouched in the dark, wet, cold and seasick.

Once, terrified by the close sound of surf, she cried out, only to be told that the boat was surrounded by porpoises. Not long afterward, they truly were in the surf, to be hauled out of danger only by frantic pulling of the oars. All through the day and the night the boat plunged and thumped. "I dreaded what the next minute might bring," she remembered, "but we still went on, the boat jumping, no one speaking, but the quick *Hard up! Hard up!* from the Captain told me too plainly how much danger we were in."

With daylight, the captain pulled the screen open so Emily could have fresh air, and when she looked out it was to see that the men were all wet through, shivering with cold and looking woebegone. A little bread and water with rum brought them round, and though the wind was freezing, the sun came out so that Wooldridge could take a sight, and they all felt a little more cheerful. But another night lay ahead.

The men curled up in the bottom of the boat, the man at the tiller being relieved every two hours. The day that followed was even colder, and the cabin boy was growing delirious. The captain ordered the oars put out, and the exercise warmed the boy a little, but then it came on to rain. Another nightfall, and another small ration of rum and water, and after another eternity of dark another morning dawned, this one brighter than the one before.

Emily insisted on changing places with her husband, so that he could take some rest in her cubby hole. Sitting up in the middle thwarts, she looked about at the men, alarmed at how aged they looked. And so, to distract them from their misery, she began to tell them stories — "of places I had visited, Gibraltar, Tangier, Cadiz and Lisbon; they listened an apparently enjoyed my descriptions." It was as if the sound of her voice, and the images of strange places that she evoked, helped them to keep on living.

And so the long, cold hours trudged by, while Emily grew hoarse. Lumps of wood drifted by, and the air was full of birds, who screamed in competition with her voice. The wind was light, and the boat sailed very, very slowly. At noon the captain was wakened to take a sight of the sun, and check their position on the chart — halfway, he reckoned; they ought to see land on Saturday, three days hence.

Again, the men were told to put out the oars and pull for warming exercise, and again night fell, with its ration of rum and water. "I noticed," wrote Emily with great misgiving, "the men's eyes were beginning to look wild."

In the morning there was just bread and water for breakfast. The men were sluggish, and the cabin boy cried when ordered to sit up and move about. Those who were not comatose wrangled with each other over the single pipe and tobacco, and all day there was nothing to be seen but sea and sky. And so the hours dragged on, until night fell once again.

Saturday dawned with mist, which made the prospect even more miserable. Despite the captain's prediction, there was no sight of land. At midday the last of the preserved meat was handed out with a little bread, and the men started to talk a little, but still in a listless manner. The water was gone, and so the only drink was the tea Emily had made so many days earlier. Some of the men, she noticed, watched her with strange, wolfish expressions on their faces. They were starving, she supposed, but the tea would have to suffice.

Sunday, and still no sight of land. It was very hard to wake the men, and Hayward had to be repeatedly ordered to get up and relieve Fielding at the tiller. Then it was found that the boat was way off course, as Fielding had gone to sleep at the helm. Bread and cold tea were handed out, and the captain tried to raise their spirits by reading from the Bible. To Emily's distress, his voice was very weak, and he had to constantly clear his throat. He improved after he had finished reading the Book of Esther, because the men began to ask him questions about what it was like to live in Arabia, and finding answers to their queries livened up his mind. Realizing that activity was best, he gave them little tasks about the boat — the main sheet needed repair where it had chafed in the block. Then it was time for Oates to take over the tiller.

A disagreeable sea was tossing the boat about, but at least the wind was in their favor. Fielding, who had the sharpest eyes, was told to keep a lookout for land. In the event, however, it was Captain Wooldridge himself who had the first sight of the Falklands. It was still far away, a blue silhouette in the distance, but when night fell they were sailing along a coast — Beauchene Island, said the captain.

And it was only just in time, as their bread was all gone.

In the morning, despite the lack of breakfast, the men's spirits were high. Shag Rock was sighted in the morning, and at noon they raised the lighthouse. To Emily, it looked amazingly grand, standing up tall with its bands of black and white, sharply silhouetted against the sea and sky. Then, as dusk fell, she saw the light flash out. She watched it pass by, mesmerized, and then she suddenly cried, "Why, there is a man coming down to the beach!"

Everyone shouted at once, so that no one could hear a word that was shouted to them, but it was obvious that the man was calling out to them to try to land through the heavy surf. Emily, terrified, begged her husband not to try it, but to make for the harbor instead, and so the men put out the oars and heaved with a will for Port Stanley.

Port Stanley! Night fell, but not before the men had seen Emily give way, at last, to emotion. "The missus is crying," said Hayward in disbelief, and as Emily indignantly wrote, "If the boat had upset, more commotion could not have been made." She denied it hotly and told them to watch instead for Wolf Rock, a dangerous sentinel on the way into the port. It was too dark to see, so the captain ordered a camphor flare lit, and it was Emily herself who glimpsed it, and told the men to steer away.

Still, no one came out to help, so they rowed doggedly on. Then their tired arms and shoulders gave out, so the sail was raised, though the breeze was against them. They were forced to constantly tack, beating against the wind to get into port. The men began to whine, so Emily gave them the last of the brandy, but when it was gone they set to complaining again. When they tried rowing again, the steward's oar caught in kelp, nearly throwing him overboard, and then when they were settled again the rudder became tangled in weed and had to be lifted out.

On they struggled. To be so close to safety and yet so

far was frustrating in the extreme. As both Emily and her husband knew already, the entrance to the harbor was very narrow, guarded on each side by high hills. Why did not one come out to help?

With a loud clap and a fizz, a rocket rose and exploded in the air, and then another. The lighthouse keeper had finally sent word of a shipwrecked crew to the harbor, perhaps. But then they saw the steamship-of-war — HMS *Pleiades*, it turned out to be. Should they steer for her? She blazed with lights. And there was music. Something was happening on board of her, so they steered for the shore.

The landing stage was attached to a hulk. There were men there, waiting for a boat. Waiting for the shipwrecked crew? No, the men said in astonished voices, eyeing the bedraggled people in the longboat. They were waiting for a boat to take them out to the *Pleiades* — there was a ball, they said. A new governor had arrived, and the whole of Port Stanley was celebrating. So that, Emily thought with disbelief, was why no one had noticed their plight. Everyone was too busy having fun.

Wearily, the men made the longboat fast, and Captain Wooldridge clambered out, saying that he would go on shore to report. He staggered as he stood on the rocking stage, and had trouble walking, so he came back for Emily, so he could use her shoulder for support. When he arrived, the men who were all dressed up for the ball had a lantern out, and were examining the castaways with curiosity.

They became quite animated when Emily crawled out of her cubby hole in response to her husband's call. A woman! A wrecked woman! When Emily tried to stand her legs gave away, so at last the men who had been standing on the stage stepped forward to help. Between them, they got her and the captain as far as the door of the only inn — but it was locked, and no one answered their cries and their knocking. The steward and the cabin boy and the three seamen had followed their captain and his wife, reluctant to stay any longer in the longboat. In the light of the lantern, Emily saw their gaunt faces, their staring eyes and utter exhaustion. The cabin boy was particularly badly off. But they all had to wait until someone came back from the ball.

One of the men who belonged to the *Pleiades* finally had the sense to go to the ballroom and find an official to take charge of the castaways — so at long last a gentleman arrived to arrange shelter and food for them all. And Captain Wooldridge, to his relief, was able to make his report. The gentleman was named Dean. It was he who at last lavished Emily and her husband with care and sympathy. He took them into his own house, while the boarding house was opened for the steward and the cabin boy and the three exhausted seamen.

Staggering inside Mr. Dean's house, Emily lurched to a stop, unable to believe her eyes. A table was set out with sparkling silver and crystal, but that was not all of it. "Oh Richard, a tablecloth!" she cried. For the first time, she truly believed she was back in civilization, and as she wrote, her heart was filled with thankfulness to God.

More sobering moments were to come. One was the first sight of her own face in a mirror — thin, brown, and gaunt, with staring eyes and wild hair. Sleepless nights and nightmares lay ahead, too, along with the mortification of depending on charity while her husband went back to Staten Island on the government schooner *Foam* to rescue Harris, Lawson and Sargent. As distressed British seamen, the men who had been marooned by the loss of the *Maid of Athens* merited two sets of clothes, along with fares back to England and some pocket money. Emily Wooldridge, on the other hand, was forced to rely on the generosity of the kind ladies of Port Stanley.

Because she was a woman, the British Government owed her nothing.

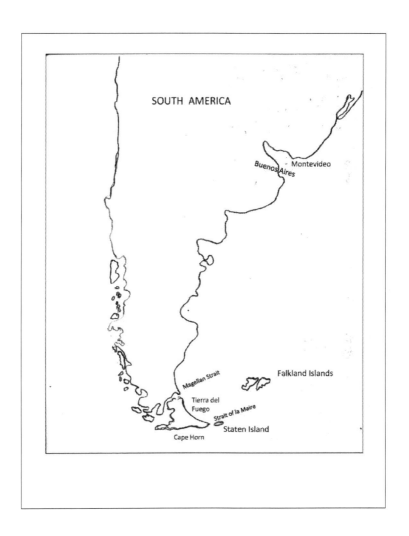

SOUTH CHINA SEA AND EAST INDIES

FOUR

Encounters with Pirates

Late at night on June 26, 1849, whaling wife Mary Brewster was trying to get some sleep, despite the worries that beset her. Her husband, Captain William Brewster, had had such bad luck in finding whales that he had taken the desperate measure of sailing into the Arctic Ocean, even though he had never been there before, and the sea was not just storm-ridden and ice-bound, but largely uncharted, too. Mary had not wanted to go there at all, but had been phlegmatic about it, though being beset by large floes of ice turned out to be nerve-wracking for them all. The moment that she totally lost her composure, however, was when Mr. Cook, the fourth officer, came rushing into the after quarters screaming, *"The bloody Indians are coming."*

Mary was so alarmed, in fact, that she — the epitome of the proper, decent, demure New England wife — actually wrote down the word "bloody" in her diary. It really was too much, she protested — "I had in a measure got use to the ice and thought we should get clear from it when the wind changed but the indians was a new subject & very unexpected." Her husband, Captain William Brewster, was equally anxious — "a few spades was got down," she wrote, meaning the razor-sharp spades that were used for cutting blubber — "four old muskets loaded neither of them though would go off — or not more than one." As it happened, the Indians were friendly Inuit people, who simply wanted to trade for tobacco, but at the time it gave them all a very nasty fright.

Mary had good reason to be panic-stricken, however. Piracy and native attack has featured in the annals of the sea ever since the first men took to boats, for stealing those boats and whatever was in them — including the people, if there was a slave market handy — was so very profitable. Stories about pirates and murderous natives were told in mead halls and around campfires, in coffee houses, and in captains' living rooms, and girls and women were just as fascinated and appalled as male listeners. It gave a spice of dread and danger to the prospect of going to sea, especially if the vessel was bound to one of the world's current hotspots of piratical attack.

While the Arctic was little known, apart from the very real danger of ice, a definite hotspot was the South China Sea. Ever since the colorful era when magnificent East Indiamen loaded deep with rich cargoes of gold, silk and immensely valuable spices plied the East Indies, that region had been notorious. In times of strife and privation, maritime looting has often been the only means of economic survival, and in the East Indies and the South China Sea not only were the people often very poor, but it was remarkably easy to get away with seizing vessels and their cargoes. As the captains of European vessels were acutely aware, long knives, spears and clubs were routinely found on native *prahus*, being tools of the fishing trade, and the friendly fisherman who had just sold them some fish and a turtle or two was all too likely to metamorphose into a pirate, if he found the ship becalmed in an otherwise empty sea.

For this reason, the men who sailed to the Spice Islands were just as nervous as the women. One such was Dr. Robert Smith Owen, surgeon of the South Seaman *Warrens,* who wrote in December 1837, while in the Makassar Strait between Borneo and the Celebes, that "here the Malay pirates are so plentiful we think it prudent therefore to prepare our guns &c. in case of a surprise." Another was Dr. John Wilson, surgeon of the London South Seas whaler *Gipsy.* "The Malays are a piratical, bloodthirsty people: under the frenzying influence of opium they execute deeds of violence & of blood!" he exclaimed in May 1840, when the *Gipsy* was cruising between Timor and Celebes (modern Sulawesi). A little later he added, "upon the little shrub covered rock called Pulo-Batto or Batto rock, a merchant-captain lies buried who was slain in defending his vessel against an attack made by a set of Malay pirates."

Grisly descriptions from fellow seafarers served to make European men and women even jumpier — and, in some cases, trigger-happy, too. In 1831, just after she arrived at the island of Celebes, Eliza, wife of Captain Michael Underwood of the South Seas whaler *Kingsdown,* was told a disturbing tale by a comprador (ships' agent) by the name of Burns, who had just come back to the port of Monado from Ambon, one of the Spice Islands, where he had been trading in muskets.

Business there had gone so well, he said, that when he had left Ambon he was carrying a large purse of silver-rich sicca rupees, and quite a lot of gold. Naturally, then, his heart had sunk when he spied "seven Maggandanna prows" steering in the direction of his leaky old schooner. As he elaborated to Eliza, these "Maggandanna" pirates (actually Ilanoan, as they hailed from Illana Bay, Mindanao) had a particularly savage reputation, for "their custom is when they take prisoners to braise their knees and elbows every day by hard blows so as to keep them too stiff to make their escape till they can dispose of them" — that is, sell them in a slave market.

Naturally, then, Mr. Burns took evasive action, steering close to the nearest shore in the hope that the pirate *prahus*, with their deeper draft, would run aground. Instead, once he was in shallow water, his entire crew jumped ship — as one man, they leaped overboard and dashed into the jungle. Aghast, Mr. Burns sat and watched as they tore into the trees, "looking on them in utter despair," and at a complete loss to know what to do.

The Ilanoan vessels hove to within gunshot, and their captains called out to him to surrender and deliver. Instead, Mr. Burns gathered his wits, a cutlass, and his rupees, and followed in the wake of his swift-heeled men. Getting onto the beach ahead of the pirates, he tore his bag of coins open, and scattered them behind him as he fled. And, "as he had hoped, they staid scrambling for the money."

It was a desperate (and expensive) ploy, but at least Mr. Burns had escaped with a whole hide. One can easily imagine Eliza Underwood clasping her hands in horror as she listened. Then, just three weeks after listening to the nerve-wracking story told by Mr. Burns, she felt a reminiscent chill. Her own crisis was close to hand, and, like the comprador, at that moment she had no idea how to cope with it.

The *Kingsdown* was very much in need of fresh fruit and vegetables for the scurvy-ridden crew, and because of this, Captain Underwood had ventured too close to one of the Lesser Sunda Islands, which was inhabited by "a very savage tribe — said to be cannables" — or so Eliza had been told. No sooner was the ship inside this most dangerous bay than the wind died down, leaving the *Kingsdown* drifting. As Eliza put it, the ship had been trapped in "a bay or bite as the sailors call it."

From the deck, Eliza could see the flames of their camp fires leaping up into the night-black sky, and the silhouettes of pirate canoes on the beach. No one was in charge of the *Kingsdown* — her husband, Michael Underwood, was confined to bed with a severe bout of gout, completely incapable of taking charge of the quarterdeck, and the mates were incompetent. On many South Seamen, the ship's surgeon was asked often to take over the deck, particularly when the whaleboats were down, but the *Kingsdown*'s doctor was useless. If those canoes set sail or paddled towards the ship, she could only hope that somehow the poor scurvy-ridden crew could keep them off with the ship's small firepower. She might even have to take charge of the guns herself.

Shaken with foreboding, Eliza went back to the cabin. "Not long after that," she wrote, "I perceived that the ship had been going about. I rushed up on deck, and to my great dismay found we were in an even worse situation than before. The breeze is so light it only just enables us to stem the current, which means that, if a calm overtakes us, we shall certainly drift in shore among the savages.

"The night was made ghastly with my trembling fears," she scribbled on. "I did not dread the pirates of Makassar nearly so much as the natives of this coast, for [they] are wild wretches who do not even spare their own race; they sacrifice life for the sheer joy of it, or to furnish their horrible meals. It is little wonder that a timid woman should dread the thought of falling into their hands."

This, the entry for Saturday, September 24, 1831, is the last in Eliza's journal. She ends, "I hope I shall close my next book with a more pleasing reflection, surely I shall for the next will close in London, but yet I have much to dread." And it is here that Eliza Underwood vanishes from the record. It is impossible to tell if she did start another book, or even survived this crisis. But, if she did return to London she most certainly had stirring tales of her own to relate to her horrorstricken friends.

As Eliza was acutely aware, native attack from shore was a definite hazard of life at sea, particularly in the tropics. Captains of ships that called at remote islands were taking definite risks when they sent parties on shore to cut firewood, fill their fresh water casks, and provision with fruits and coconuts. Even if the same natives had traded in a friendly fashion a year or so before, danger could be lurking. A dishonest or trigger-happy European captain just might have called in the meantime, and natives who had been cheated or slaughtered were all too likely to wreak revenge on the next vessel that called, no matter how innocent that particular captain might be.

This happened so often that stories of native treachery and massacre ran about the salons and saloons even more readily than tales of pirates. There was, for instance, the well publicized wreck of the *Flying Fox* on a reef at Nonouti — in what was known then as the Gilbert Islands — in the year 1851. No sooner was the vessel pinned and helpless than the natives swarmed on board for plunder, and Captain Brown saved his wife only by disguising her as a man — or so it was reported.

Equally chilling was the story of the American ship *Henrietta,* which on June 7, 1860 was anchored off picture-perfect Santa Isabel, in the Solomon Islands. All was so tranquil and non-threatening that Captain Brown sent a boat with the carpenter and five men on shore. Their job was to cut firewood and a couple of spars, but instead they met disaster. Only one of the woodcutting party returned on board, swimming frantically across the lagoon and then scrambling on deck to relate the ghastly news of a "fearful outrage," of which he was the only survivor. As the *Daily Evening Traveler* of Boston related, "The man, who swam to the ship from the shore informed him (the master) that they had been attacked and murdered by the natives of the island."

Even worse was to come. "Shortly afterward the ship was suddenly boarded by a number of natives, who attempted to take forcible possession." This was not easy to repel — Captain Brown was at a grave disadvantage, as the loss of five men had so drastically reduced his crew. As the report went on, there was just himself, the cook, and four seamen on board, this last including the poor, shocked fellow who had just swum back with the terrible tidings. Brown did not count his wife and two children, who were also there, because in the heat of the moment he did not have time to think of them.

Within seconds of the invasion he was grappled by the natives, and it was only after a desperate struggle that he managed to break away and escape to the deck cabin where the firearms were stowed. Foiled, the natives "next attacked his wife, who also succeeded in escaping their vengeance, and sought refuge with her husband in the cabin, where they kept up a constant firing on the natives."

As well as being resourceful, Mrs. Brown must have been an excellent shot, for she managed to drive the natives away. Jumping into their canoes, "they made off, carrying with them one of the children, a fine little boy about five years old." Hastily making sail, Captain Brown pursued the canoes in the hope of rescuing his son, but was unsuccessful.

The Browns never saw the little boy again.

It is no surprise, then, that the new bride of Captain Alonzo Follansbee got quite a shock when she first viewed the furnishings of the captain's cabin on his ship. It was May 1837, and she had just boarded the Boston merchantman *Logan* for her honeymoon voyage — and there, facing her as she walked into the cabin, was a complete wall "lined with muskets, pistols, cutlasses and boarding pikes."

When she gasped in stunned surprise, her husband merely simply remarked in a casual fashion that the weaponry was necessary, as they were bound to the South China Sea. And that was all the explanation necessary. Having read the journals and shipping lists, Nancy Follansbee knew exactly what that destination implied. So, being a practical woman, she took precautions — which turned out to be no good at all.

She found this out, much to her discomfiture, just eleven months later. The *Logan* was lying becalmed in the Straits, the wind having died. The sails hung as limp as washing on a line, and the ship rolled slowly in the mirror-like turquoise sea. If danger threatened, it was impossible to take any kind of evasive action. Therefore it came as a most unpleasant shock when the lookout suddenly hollered that a pirate *prahu* was bearing down on them.

It was dawn on April 22, 1838. "*Pirate vessel in sight!*" he shouted.

And when they all looked, it was to see the pirate

prahu coming up with astonishing speed, paddled by lines of powerful native seamen. "Our cannon, swivel guns and pistols were soon got in readiness," Nancy Follansbee wrote; "swords, cutlasses, boarding pikes and ammunition hustled on deck ready for them."

By five in the afternoon the ship was still becalmed and helpless, and the pirates were less than a mile away. Nancy, however, allowed herself to feel a measure of self-congratulation, because, as she wrote, she "had practiced loading and firing guns and pistols at targets all the way out." But that, sadly, was also the moment when she learned it was unlikely to do her any good whatsoever. Her husband grimly informed her that her marksmanship "would be of little use." Even more depressingly, he went on to meditate in remarkably Victorian terms that once she fell into pirate hands, her fate "would be worse than death."

But, by the grace of God, she was spared that melodramatic fate — "a good breeze sprang up, and we were soon out of their reach," and Nancy sailed on, to become the mother of the first American baby born in the Celestial Kingdom.

Charlotte, wife of Captain David Babcock of the famous clipper *Young America,* was another American woman to have a brush with Oriental pirates, and a very unusual one, too. The adventure began in late 1854, when Charlotte was on shore in Shanghai, where she had been left by her husband to give birth to her third baby daughter. All went well, but when the baby was about a month old, David sent

Charlotte a message, instructing her to charter a steam tug, and travel with it to Ning-Po, an opium port where he was waiting with the ship.

While this seems no small mission, Charlotte was a seasoned seafaring wife, so had no trouble carrying it out. She hired a steamboat that turned out to be captained by man by the name of Thomas W. Dearborn, who carried his wife, Mary, and their own small daughter. This meant that Charlotte and her little girls could expect good company, which should make the passage up the coast all that more pleasant. Unfortunately, however, Mary Dearborn was violently seasick, leaving Charlotte in charge of all the children.

Worse still, when they arrived at Ning-Po it was to find that the *Young America* had sailed. A favorable wind had sprung up, so David Babcock had decided to go ahead without waiting for his family. The steamboat and the clipper must have passed each other in the night, which meant that the *Young America* was presumably close to making port in Shanghai. Glumly, Captain Dearborn turned back. Not only had he lost his towage fee, but he was stuck with Mrs. Babcock and her undoubtedly fractious family.

Then, however, he was intercepted by a Chinese vessel that was flying a flag of distress. The Chinese captain could speak no English, and Dearborn had very little Chinese, but the river pilot he had just taken on board the steamboat was able to translate, and so Thomas Dearborn learned not just that a Chinese merchant on board the ship had been robbed of a bag of gold, but also that the pirate junk was still in sight.

With no more ado, and despite Charlotte's protests about the risks, not to mention the waste of time and money, he chugged off in pursuit of the pirate, and shortly afterward brought the junk to with one shot across the bows. That the pirate junk made no attempt to fight back should be enough to make any cynical shipmaster suspect that perhaps it was not a pirate at all. Charlotte Babcock, however, felt no doubts. "A more villainous set of faces I never saw," she declared after the twenty-two-strong crew of the junk was paraded on the deck. And the Chinese merchant was hugely delighted, exclaiming "Hi yah!" when his bag of gold was rummaged out from where it had been hidden.

His joy was short-lived. When the merchant called out that it was to be thrown to him, a mighty heave was made, but the heavy bag fell short, and with a splash and a plop it disappeared into the depths. His plunge into despair, according to Charlotte's description, was as deep as the water. Then, while he was loudly mourning his loss, two of the pirates jumped overboard and drowned themselves, much to Captain Dearborn's chagrin, as live pirates were worth a bounty.

He steamed back to Ning-Po to hand over the remaining twenty, despite Charlotte's renewed remonstrations. She was the person who had hired the steamboat, and she wanted to join her husband, wherever he might be! But Captain Dearborn paid no heed at all, being determined to make some kind of profit from the venture. Mrs. Babcock soon relaxed, however, there was not much delay at all. Within hours of arriving at Ning-Po the pirates had all been beheaded, and Thomas Dearborn was able to weigh anchor.

As Charlotte remarked in matter-of-fact tones after they chugged away, "Chinese justice is summary."

FIVE

The Living Age

Another American clipper captain's wife to have an unusual passing brush with Oriental pirates was Mrs. Robert P. Holmes. And whether those pirates were real or not was again a matter for debate — though the seamen certainly believed in them.

The ship was the clipper *Living Age*, and the captain was Robert P. Holmes, while the second mate was a young man by the name of Frederic Hinckley. As Hinckley reminisced later, the voyage was unlucky from the day they left New York. Luckily, the *Living Age* was a fine, staunch ship, for the passage about Cape Horn was long and arduous. They beat against contrary gales for thirty days, battling snow and sleet and ice while the stock of provisions and fresh water ran so low that everyone had to be put on short rations. Scurvy appeared in the forecastle, and one of the seamen died. Another fell from the ice-slicked rigging while struggling to reef the main topsail, striking the rail with an audible thud on the way. Even if he had survived the plunge into the icy sea, it was impossible to lower a boat in the midst of the gale. And so his name became another sad entry in the logbook.

One hundred and fifty-two days after leaving New York, the ship finally dropped anchor in Honolulu, where she discharged her mixed cargo. Captain Holmes could not find a return freight, so he sailed for Shanghai to pick up a consignment of teas and silks — a cargo that some of the papers valued at the immense sum of three hundred thousand dollars. He also had to pick up seamen. The ones who had come on the outward voyage reckoned they weren't willing to face the storms of Cape Stiff again, and took their discharge in the Chinese port, so Holmes was forced to ship an almost entirely new crew. Oddly, one of the new men, a mariner from Genoa, got cold feet, "and left us from sheer superstitious fear that the old ship would come to grief," Frederic Hinckley, the staunch young second mate, wrote. As he meditated, no one could tell why the Genoese had jumped to that conclusion, but it was a dire presage of what was to come.

The *Living Age* weighed anchor from Shanghai on Christmas Day, 1855. As Hinckley remembered, there were "twenty-three souls on board: Captain Holmes and his wife, three mates, and eighteen men and boys before the mast." The new crew was as mixed as the old cargo, comprising Americans, Englishmen, a couple of Swedes, one Italian, and a cook who was French. Mixed as they were, though, Hinckley reckoned them "an excellent set of sailors." But, as events were to demonstrate, they were as superstitious as the Genoese.

It was the season of the northeast monsoon, so the winds were favorable as the ship flew south, but at the same time the weather brought thick fog. Right in their way as they entered the South China Sea, steering to the west of the Philippines, was a horseshoe-shaped island named Pratas. Though its sheltered inlet was a resort for Chinese boats in the fishing season, the island was uninhabited, so without lights or buoys. It was also no more than thirty feet high at it greatest elevation, so sighting it before the ship hit it was a challenge for the lookouts. Worst of all, the island was rimmed for forty miles in every direction by a reef that was known as the Pratas Shoal. Unsurprisingly, as Hinckley said, it was a trap for sailing ships — "Many a noble ship has laid her bones thereon." And, in that fog, it was almost impossible to see anything of the reef until the island was almost under a ship's counter. Naturally, then, when second mate Hinckley took over the deck on the fifth night out, when they were nearing the shoal, he was distinctly nervous.

Being a clipper, the *Living Age* was not going slowly. Instead, she was bowling along under rather a lot of canvas — double-reefed fore and mizzen topsails, a main topsail with only one reef, and fully set main topgallant sail and foresail. This meant that when Hinckley glimpsed what he thought might be a breaker, and rushed forward with his heart in his mouth, it was too late to do anything about it.

Before he was halfway to the bows, the ship brought up on the coral with a crash. "The halyards were all let go fore and aft" — but to no effect, as the sails stayed full, making it impossible to lower the yards. In effect, the *Living Age* was doing her utmost to sail across the reef, but was banging up and down with tremendous force, instead.

It looked as if the bottom would give way and the ship would go down in moments. Captain Holmes shouted, "Lower the boats!" — but before the seamen could even reach them. a tremendous wave smashed through the bulwarks, washing everything off the deck that had not been lashed down, including the boats. When it washed back, it unshipped the rudder, so that the tiller swung back and forth, wiping still more gear overboard. Another wave, and the after part of the hull broke and slumped, so that the bow was high in the air.

Another order was given, and axes were frantically

fetched, and the topmasts cut away, but still the ship pounded down on the rocks with every surging wave. The next step was to cut through the foremast level with the deck — but at that moment dawn glimmered on the horizon, and to the crew's horror, they thought they saw a pirate ship. "It seemed a large boat crowded with men, standing up, motionless, with cruel eyes glaring," wrote Hinckley. And, as everyone knew, "In those seas at that period all Chinese wreckers and fishermen could be classed as incarnate fiends who thirsted for the blood of all foreigners."

Someone screamed, *"The pirates are waiting for daylight to come aboard!"* Panic reigned. One old man, white hair streaming in the wind, stood up on a spar singing and shrieking in a hysterical fit, while other men hammered on the door to the after quarters, demanding liquor so they could drink themselves into insensibility before they were slaughtered. And then they were abruptly brought up short by the appearance of a very strange figure.

The only man who was not surprised at the sudden sight was Frederic Hinckley, the second mate. As he related another time, while the men had been cutting down the topmasts he had rushed below to his cabin in the after quarters, intending to take off the sodden clothes he wore under his oilskins, in case he was forced to swim for his life. There, he found Mrs. Holmes calmly sitting on a sea chest, clad in a pair of her husband's pants, and the first mate's coat and vest.

When she heard Hinckley's hurrying steps, she looked up. With eyebrows raised she inquired, "Do you have a ditty box?"

A ditty box was a seaman's store of such useful things as soap, tobacco, scissors, and needles and thread. "Yes," said Hinckley, and took down the box from a shelf in his stateroom. Then, as he related, "Mrs. Holmes, as calmly as if she had been in her own sitting room, selected from the box needles and thread, which she carefully tucked away in the pockets of her coat" — and all this while the ship was lurching and the bottom was pounding against coral.

Then she said, "You don't happen to have an extra hat, do you?"

Frederic was able to help her out with that too, as he had what he called a "Louis Kossuth hat," which was a Hungarian winter hat with ear flaps that could be tied beneath the chin. Looking pleased, Mrs. Holmes set to cutting her hair short with his scissors, and after it was cropped close to her head she pulled on the hat, tied it under her chin, and reckoned she was ready.

"There, don't I look like a boy?" she said, standing up — and, after picking up a dirk and shoving it into her belt, she walked calmly up the companionway and onto the deck.

And the panic and commotion ceased. The men all stopped their noise, staring in utter disbelief. This meant that when a lookout shouted out that the so-called pirate ship was in fact just the ruins of a very old wreck, they could hear what he said. Shuffling about sheepishly, they all laughed at themselves and each other. More importantly still, because of Mrs. Holmes' example of bravery and coolness they were all shamed into a glimmer of optimism, and set to clearing up the wreckage with a will.

Through throwing anything loose and unnecessary overboard, they were managing to get the ship lightened, but still to no effect. The after part of the clipper began to collapse, and the breakers were washing into the hold, tearing at the cargo. It looked as if the *Living Age* would break up very soon, so men were set to salvaging provisions, while another gang began to build a raft out of spars. But it all seemed hopeless. There was no chance of getting away, as the surf was too high, and the weather was getting worse. As the hours of the day crept by the gale rose, and the fog came down, and all the time the hull hammered slowly on the reef.

Night came. Captain, wife and crew gathered on the forecastle deck, the highest part of the ship. A bed was made for Mrs. Holmes by laying boards between the windlass and a barrel, and a sail hung up to give her a modicum of privacy and shelter. The men huddled together on the deck trying to snatch some sleep, but were too drenched to rest. It is easy to imagine Captain Holmes' state of mind — would the ship break up in the night, casting them all into the water?

The hours of foreboding were punctuated by the grim slam, slam, slam of the hull on the reef. But, in the morning, miraculously, the bow was still holding together. Indeed, the gale had blown the fore part of the ship higher up on the reef, onto a crest of coral where it was out of reach of the breakers. And so the men set back to work, salvaging provisions and working on the raft, all the time trying to ignore the gale that relentlessly stormed on.

Sunday January 4, 1856, dawned bright and sunny, for a wonder, and they all perked up — in time to see a ship pass them by, close enough to hear the sound of her progress, completely ignoring their plight even though they flew distress banners made from silk that had been in the cargo. This made them even more desperate to get off the wreck and onto the island, and at last the first raft was ready. Twelve volunteers stepped on board of it, led by the first officer, Mr. Campbell. To the vast relief of those who were left behind on board, the raft sailed safely into smooth water, and then, slowly, crept out of sight, driven by its single sail and steered by oars. Would they make the island? The arrangement was that those on the wreck would light a lantern when night fell, and the volunteers would light their own fire in response, but to the intense disappointment of those on the wreck, there was nothing to be seen. Glumly, as the dark night drew on, they gave up their shipmates as lost.

Next morning, the gale was back. Knowing that despair would come with idleness, Captain Holmes set the men back to work, some building a second raft, and others constructing a boat out of the ceiling boards of his cabin. When a cask of English ale was discovered, he allowed them to drink it. One man got very drunk, having snared more than his share, but it did not prove the problem that it could have been, as the tipsy fellow's antics made them all laugh. And then, providentially, Mrs. Holmes' wind-up music box was also discovered. It was damaged by salt water, but still had a few tunes in its innards. From then on they kept it wound up and playing constantly, as the music was so cheerful — until the day, that is, that it gave up the ghost. "Its last note fled, and we gave it a sailor's burial," wrote the young second mate.

For some reason the demise of the music box was the trigger for another bout of despair. The men went in a delegation to the captain, asking permission to abandon ship. Robert Holmes flatly refused, saying it was needlessly dangerous when the boat was so nearly finished. When he pointed out that his wife was content to stay on board, and she cheerfully backed him up in this, the wreck the men caved in and went away. As Frederic Hinckley pointed out, Mrs. Holmes had been an example of constancy and heroism throughout their perils and hardships. Indeed, as he frankly admitted, all the men and officers adored her. And now, in face of her cool and calm example, the men were ashamed of their cowardice.

Then the boat was finished, but the sea was still too rough to risk putting it down on the water, so Captain Holmes kept them busy fitting it out with a mast and sail, brass rowlocks, and oars made from capstan bars. That done, they filled in more time by ornamenting the boat with the fancy bits of gilded wooden "gingerbread" that had decorated the ship. Then another boat was built, a much smaller one, and a large raft to carry provisions was finished.

On the twentieth morning after the wreck they sighted another ship — "so near that we could distinguish the man at the wheel, others loosing the mainsail, and the officer of the watch pacing the deck." Frantically, the seamen ran up all the bunting they could, and stood on the highest part of the bow, shouting and waving their hats. But, like the other ship, the stranger passed by without the slightest acknowledgement.

It was probably not surprising that after that trouble arose with the crew. The trouble was a farcical one — the French cook, who was evidently a sea lawyer as well as a chef, knew that according to maritime law his pay stopped the day his ship was wrecked, and he had been brooding about it. And, forthwith, he devised a rule of his own — of no pay, no work. In a word, he refused to cook.

Well, said the men, they had been building the boats and two rafts while he had been cooking, and they weren't being paid, either. So, by logic, if he didn't do his own work, then he didn't deserve to benefit from theirs. Accordingly, there would be no place for him on either the boats or the raft when they attempted to get on shore. The Frenchman, after thinking deeply about this, decided to make his own getaway vehicle, but all he could manage was a washtub lashed between two pieces of spar. This proved so obviously unseaworthy (along with the men's derisive laughter), that he gave up his one-man strike, and went back to his proper work in the galley.

The fourth Sunday dawned with comparatively moderate weather, so the carpenter and a whaleman from New London named Coleman volunteered to try out the smaller boat, which the builders had named *Saucy Lucy*. With immense care *Saucy Lucy* was lowered overboard in slings, braced by the two men inside her. Then she set off — and that night the party on the wreck saw a light on the island, and were able to celebrate the knowledge that Coleman and the carpenter had made it on shore.

Then, however, the gale sprung up again, and did not moderate until February 4, 1856, the thirty-fifth day after the wreck of the clipper *Living Age*. On that memorial day, to everyone's immense surprise, a Chinese sampan hove into view, manned by the carpenter, Coleman, and two of the first mate's volunteers. So Mr. Campbell and his men had not drowned, after all! As they soon found out, Mr. Campbell had indeed lit the pre-arranged fire. It was just that the party on the wreck had missed their signals.

They approached the wreck, but there was no way the sampan could survive the breakers that surrounded the *Living Age* where she stood on the reef. Men shouted, signals were flown, but communication was impossible — until someone thought of the Frenchman's washtub, which had meantime been christened *Cook's Folly*. This was launched at the end of a rope, and as the rope was let out it drifted up to the anchored sampan. One man got into the tub, and was hauled up to the *Living Age*, and so, one by one, all four brave men were back with their erstwhile companions. As Hinckley said, "Passengers from a voyage around the world could not have been more heartily welcomed."

Spirits were even further boosted by the sight of another ship — the third. And this one backed her sails and lowered a boat — but sounds of a sudden commotion on the stranger echoed across the water, and the boat hurriedly returned. To the disbelief of those on the bow of the *Living Age*, the sails of the other ship filled, and she passed swiftly out of sight. Something had happened. But what? Why raise their hopes and then dash them again? It seemed so unnecessarily cruel.

Captain Holmes and his wife advised the men to put the thoughts out of their minds, and to concentrate on getting ready to abandon ship. The boat and the raft were almost ready when another sail was raised — the fourth ship to arrive. She came closer, closer — and then to everyone's horror it was realized that she was bearing straight for the reef. Signals were frantically flown, but night fell without any acknowledgement or deviation from course. The dark hours passed in suspense, and when morning came it was to see that their worst fears were justified. The other ship lay on the reef about six miles distant, still with her canvas fully set. Silently, the *Living Age* castaways watched as her boats were lowered, and then they pulled away. Soon, they thought, they would have company. But no one arrived.

On February 6, 1856, the wreck of the *Living Age* was abandoned. The whole party set sail in the remaining boat, the sampan, and the raft, carrying all the provisions they had salvaged with them, and so they left the *Living Age* forever. The passage through the reefs was nerve-wracking in the extreme, but in the morning they landed, rejoining Mr. Campbell and his other two men. Mrs. Holmes was one of the last to be ferried to shore, ceremoniously carried to the beach.

Being on land was a strangely foreign feeling. They had all become so accustomed to the thump, thump, thump of the wreck on the reef that they only noticed it now because of its absence. Instead, there was the rhythmic thud of the surf, but that was almost as disturbing, as it was so heavy at times that it seemed to be shaking the island. It was odd, too, to be on a level surface, and it was a long time before any of them could walk a steady straight line. Getting comfortable was not easy either, despite the tents they set up. Not only was the island overrun by rats and scorpions, but the only drinkable water had to be dug out of the sand, and was bitter and brackish.

There was the uncomfortable reminder, too, that the fishing season was near, and that it would bring a fleet of Chinese vessels. Again the seamen voiced genuine worries of being slaughtered or enslaved — and the prospect of what would happen to Mrs. Holmes if the Celestials found out her sex was too horrible to be contemplated. To reinforce these fears, there was plenty of evidence of past Chinese visitors. There was a garlic garden, evidently cultivated each year that the fleet arrived, and paths with little signposts bearing Chinese characters. Walking cautiously along these, the men made a grisly discovery — that the interior of the island was littered with human skeletons. The victims of pirates? Or other castaways? It was impossible to tell. Worse still, one of the men found a mound, and excitedly fetched a spade, imagining the pirate treasure that might lie hidden underneath the dirt. But instead of pieces of eight, he dug up a grinning corpse.

More mundane, though still disturbing, was the locating of yet another wreck. This turned out to be the ship *Thomas Chadwick*, which had gone ashore in a typhoon some months before. Coincidentally, it was owned by the same firm that owned the *Living Age*. The crew, it seemed, had lived on the island for a while, but then they had been rescued. Some of the men now asked Captain Holmes for permission to explore the wreck, which was almost high and dry in the lagoon, and this was readily given. So off they went — and were a long time returning.

It was two days before their boat came back, and then the whole camp heard them coming before they saw them. The man in the bow was shouting at the man who was at the tiller through a huge speaking trumpet, and the oarsmen were singing at the tops of their voices, wonderfully cheerful considering that their oars kept on getting tangled up. In a word, they were drunk. Having discovered the *Chadwick*'s spirit room, they "had enjoyed a regular sailor's spree," as Hinckley phrased it. They were easily forgiven, though, as they had brought back a load of canned meats, lime juice, clothing, and other useful things.

On the other hand, one of their number was missing, having decided not to come back to the camp. He preferred the prospect of life on board the wreck with its abundance of luxuries, he said, and it had been impossible to argue him out of the idea. Shrugging, his companions had left him to it. And so he lived in solitary splendor until Captain Holmes eventually sent a boat for him.   His rescuers found a profoundly grateful man, the lonesome, spooky nights having preyed on his mind, despite being bolstered with spirits.

The booty from the *Chadwick* had been so useful, though, that the second mate asked the captain if he could take a party out to the ship that they had watched in horror as it had sailed onto the reef. This permission was easily given, too. It was a struggle to get on board of her, because of the breakers on the reef, but one man braved the sharks to swim over to the wreck, and hauled up the boat with the rope he had taken with him. She was the *Tom Bowline*, and, incredibly, she was also owned by the same firm of merchants, who were bound to be smarting badly at the loss of three of their ships.

The men were able to retrieve a few provisions, but though they found guns, there was no ammunition. What had happened to her men? Later, Hinckley learned that they had rowed to China, rather than try to get to the island. If they had been trying to avoid pirates, it was a very bad choice. Most of them had been murdered as they landed, and the few who managed to escape the massacre had only got to Macao after much trouble and privation.

The *Tom Bowline* was a spooky sight in the moonlight as they sailed away from the wreck — "her full cargo of tea undamaged, all her sails set, motionless, a ghostly phantom." Then, when Hinckley and his men got back to the camp, it was to find that the mate had left in the sampan the day before, with a crew of four men.

The camp party that was left behind must have watched the boat bob out of sight with a great deal of misgiving. According to Captain Holmes' calculations, it was 160 miles, and a very dangerous journey, at that. Would they make it? Mrs. Holmes was certain they would — and made herself a shore-going dress to prove it. The gown was made out of silk from the cargo, stitched with the needles and thread the second mate had given her, and was resplendent indeed. She took off her castaway suit in her tent, and paraded out in a dress that would have given "great credit to the dressmaking trade of Pratas, and charmed the rude sailors," wrote young Frederic, who was hopelessly enchanted himself, being more than half in love with the captain's wife.

Mrs. Holmes' optimism was justified. On February 25, the plume from the smokestack of a steamer was raised on the horizon. Briskly, the steamboat made the island, dropped her anchor, and lowered a boat — and so, to their "unspeakable relief," the castaways soon found themselves on a friendly deck. Their rescuer was the English steamer *Shanghai* from Manila, commanded by Captain Munroe.

He had come in response to a report made by no one less than the captain of the ship that had lowered a boat, then taken it up again, and then sailed away. The imprecations they had sent after him had been misplaced. What they had not known — or so they now found — was that he had touched on the reef and sprung a leak, and so the boat's crew had been recalled to man the pumps. And, after that, he hadn't dared hang about, needing to get to port before his own ship sank. He limped into Manila, where he had found the Peninsula and Oriental Company *Shanghai* already steamed up, ready for departure. And Captain Munroe hadn't hesitated even a moment before setting his course for the island.

Naturally, while they were both highly relieved at the timely reprieve, Captain Holmes and his wife felt worried about the fate of the mate and his men in the sampan — but then another steamer appeared on the horizon. Briskly, it too stood off the reef, and glad signals were exchanged with Munroe and his crew, who were still busy with the rescue. As Captain and Mrs. Holmes soon found out, the mate had arrived in Hong Kong on February 17, after an eventless two-day voyage, and this second steamer had been sent in response to his report. And so, as the second mate meditated, the *Living Age* castaways had been rescued twice in the same day.

And Mrs. Holmes? As young Hinckley lyrically enthused, she had been cool and calm throughout the ordeal — "Neither the discomfort of the situation nor the prospect of death had drawn from her a sign of fear of accent of complaint." Not only was she brave and uncomplaining, but she had been determinedly cheerful throughout, urging the despondent ones never to give up hope. Was she as cool and calm as ever, as she shook Captain Munroe's hand? Was she wearing her splendid shore-going gown? Did she rustle and shimmer in a cloud of silk? It seems very likely, because there is no record of her breaking down with relief.

But she must have been close to it — for once she got home she stayed there, and never went back to sea.

SIX

Mary Ellen Clarke

"By the arrival on Wednesday of the Union Company's Royal mail steamer *German* at Southamption, a terrible tale of mutiny and murder on the high seas has reached this country, five deaths having been caused in connection therewith, and desperate injury to as many more," headlined the *News of the World* on February 7, 1886.

The victims, as the story went on to describe, were all members of the crew of the American square-rigger *Frank N. Thayer,* a crack 1547-ton vessel built in Newburyport in 1878, and owned by the Boston merchants Thayer & Lincoln. Despite the large size of the ship, the crew was relatively small, numbering just nineteen. The mate was a solid, reliable fellow by the name of Holmes, and the captain was thirty-nine year old Robert Kinnard Clarke, junior. With Clarke were his wife, Mary Ellen, also thirty-nine, and their youngest child, five-year-old Carrie. As a writer for the New York *World Telegram* marveled almost fifty years later, in May 1934, Mary Ellen had sailed with her husband ever since her marriage (at the age of twenty-one), declaring that "a wife's place was with her husband, wherever he went, and whatever befell him." Her 1909 obituary in the *Brooklyn Daily Eagle* said much the same thing — "Mr. Clarke was captain of a large sailing vessel, and his wife and children accompanied him all over the world." On the *Frank N. Thayer* voyage, however, their two sons had been left behind in Port Chester, New York.

According to the story in the *New York Times*, which was published on February 23, 1886, Clarke was an impressive looking man — "a middle-sized man of strong build," with a full black beard and a darkly tanned face, "which seems to express great determination." Mary Ellen was a small woman, with "a mild, patient face," presumably expressing a very patient nature — which is not surprising, considering some of the happenings she must have witnessed in the past, on the ships that her husband commanded. Her obituary remarked that her "experiences were many and varied," which was a drastic understatement. In those days, with steam competing with sail, and the driving need to make fast, profitable voyages as cheaply as possible, the masters and mates of downeasters were infamous for treating their crews badly. There were several whose names appeared with some regularity in the California report of brutality at sea, the *Red Record,* and Captain Robert Kinnard Clarke jr. was one of them.

Back in 1873, after the clipper *Sunrise* arrived at San Francisco from Liverpool, reports of Captain Clarke's excessive brutality had flown around town. Accusations from members of his crew led to his prosecution and conviction, followed by fourteen months in the San Francisco county jail, plus a fine of one thousand dollars. As the *Daily Alta California* reflected later, on February 2, 1886, after erroneously reporting Robert K. Clarke's death, "The trials of Clarke and his two mates, Harris and Maloney in 1873, are matters still fresh in the minds of San Francisco.

"Shortly after the arrival of the *Sunrise* in the summer

of 1873, Clarke and the two officers above named were arrested on charges of cruelty to the crew," it continued. "The three were tried by juries before Judges Sawyer and Hoffman, and no criminal trials in this city ever attracted more attention, nor were criminals ever regarded with greater indignation." Captain Clarke was convicted on seven of the fourteen counts against him, and Harris on twenty-four. Maloney pleaded guilty, and was given two months in jail, that turned out to be a death sentence, as he died while inside.

"The testimony brought out during the trials of Clarke and Harris showed a series of brutalities practiced on the *Sunrise* crew equal to anything ever described in that line by sensational nautical writers of fiction," the reporter meditated. It does seem that Clarke's first officer, Frank Harris, must have carried out most of the violence, though, and that opinions of Clarke's guilt were divided about town, because there was "great indignation" expressed when Captain Clarke was taken from the courtroom to the jail in shackles. Harris was punished much more severely than his captain, too, being sentenced for four years in the State prison — though, strangely enough, he was pardoned just before he had served out his sentence and shortly after that he joined the San Francisco police force under an alias. And, after Clarke was released from jail he was given back the command of the ship, which, meantime, had made a voyage with his father, Robert Clarke, senior, in charge. None-theless, afterward he was known the world over as "Sunrise" Clarke, which implies that his reputation for brutality stayed with him — and that Mary Ellen (who was with him on the *Sunrise* voyage) must have had a phlegmatic outlook on life, as well as being very patient.

As the *New York Times* observed, "No one would select her as a heroine." However, the disaster that befell the *Frank N. Thayer* in the South Atlantic on January 2, 1886 proved her to be brave and resourceful, as well as understanding.

On November 1, 1885, Clarke had taken his departure from Manila, in the Philippine Islands, after loading with ten thousand bales of hemp for the rope-lofts of New York. Two of his foremast hands had jumped ship in port, and so he had hired two Malay seamen to make up the deficiency. They turned out to be good seamen, and everything went well, with favorable winds across the Indian Ocean, and a smooth doubling of the Cape of Good Hope.

Then, though, there had been a fuss over medicine, as the retrospective report in the *World Telegram* described. One of the Malays had reported to the cabin with a stomach ache, but when Clarke fixed him a tumbler of salts, the seaman had taken only one taste before flatly refusing to swallow it down. A solid thump with a rope had persuaded the seaman otherwise, and the medicine had gone down "fast enough," as the journalist wrote. But when the Malay went off, he carried a hot grievance with him, which simmered inside in the place where his stomach ache had burned.

Clarke put the matter out of his mind, so that it was completely forgotten by the time New Year's Day came around. That evening he went up on deck, to find that all was well. As he told the reporter from the *New York Times*, it was a beautiful moonlight night, with a smooth sea, and the ship was cutting along handsomely on the breast of the southeast trade winds. So, after consulting with the mate, Mr. Holmes, and informing him that there was no need to call into the island of St. Helena, the ship being so well stocked, Clarke stepped down to the after cabin, washed up in his little bathroom, and then went into his stateroom, got into his night clothes, and joined Mary Ellen, who was already in bed.

He was woken at midnight by an incoherent cry. Perhaps, he thought, the mate was teaching one of the seamen a lesson, and it was an ordinary matter of discipline. However, the strangeness of the cry communicated enough urgency to get him out of bed and up the forward companionway to deck, still in his nightwear. To Clarke's horror, as he related later, the second mate, William Davies, came falling down the stairs, blood gushing from his wounds — "and with a terrible cry to me — *Captain Clarke, Captain Clarke!* — he dropped dead."

Unaware that the first mate was also mortally wounded, and had staggered into the forecastle with the intention of rousing the seamen, Captain Clarke ran up the stairway to summon him and find out what had happened. Just as he reached the top step, a blurred shape rose out of the night, and whacked him across the forehead with a sharp blade. Clarke collapsed, but before he hit the deck a strong hand gripped him about the throat. Dazed and blinded, the captain struggled to tear free. Blinking away blood, he saw that it was one of the Malays.

Forcing the man's hand away from his throat, he grappled him to the deck. A sharp movement and a burning sensation told him he had been stabbed in the arm, but still he fought, even when he slipped in his own blood and the mate's, and fell down the stairs, taking the Malay with him. Another stab of the knife as the Malay fought free — this time into Clarke's left side. Blood gushed, and Clarke crashed the rest of the way, into the corridor at the bottom. At that, the Malay ran back up the stairs, "leaving me, as he thought, dead."

Then came a slam as the mutineer shut and barricaded the door at the top of the companionway, barring way out to the amidships deck. Clarke struggled to his feet, and lurched into the after cabin. Mary Ellen was already there, roused by the noises of the struggle — as the *New York Times* reported, "In the dim light of the cabin she saw her husband stagger in completely covered with blood. She ran to him and putting her arms around him led him to the sofa. Then she rushed to the berth, and hurriedly taking one of the sheets, tore this into bandages, with which she quickly dressed his wounds." Those wounds were awful. Not only was Clarke horribly slashed about the head and arm, but the gash in his side had penetrated so deeply that the lower lobe of his left lung stuck out. After pushing it back, Mary Ellen bound a strip of sheet tightly about his chest to hold everything inside his ribs, and then sewed it in place. As Robert Clarke said later, "My wife saved my life by quick attendance to my wounds."

And all the time the terrible sounds of battle were echoing from above, evidence of the scene of carnage that was taking place on deck. The Malays had chosen their moment well, as it was the change of watch, and the seamen on duty were moving away from their stations, intent on going to bed, while others were coming on deck to relieve them. This confused movement lurched to a stop when the two Malays plunged out of the dark, shouting that the mates and captain were dead, and that they were taking over the ship.

Then the slaughter recommenced. The first man murdered was the carpenter, a German by the name of Booth. After slashing him repeatedly, they threw him overboard, and then rushed at a cluster of eight seamen on the foredeck, who gave little resistance, being stunned by the violence and speed of the assault. As a seaman by the name of Robert Sanborn testified, four were badly wounded before anyone realized what was happening.

Six, including the stabbed ones, retreated to the forecastle, where they were brought up short by the sight of the first mate lying in a pool of blood. Then, before anyone could do anything to prevent it, the two Malays slammed the forecastle door and barred it, trapping them inside. Sanborn and the eighth seaman, a man named Louis Hendrickson, escaped by running aft. Reaching the quarterdeck, Sanborn jumped onto the bulwarks and scooted up the shrouds to the mizzen crossjack yard, while Hendrickson ran down the after companionway stairs. There, a further shock awaited, as he was confronted by the ghostly figure of Captain Clarke, the white bandages bound round his head glimmering in the dim light.

It was a miracle that Clarke was alive, let alone up and moving. After Mary Ellen had tied the last stitch, he had insisted that she should help him get dressed. Then Clarke had found and loaded a revolver, and now he was ready to defend his ship. At that confused second, he was about to shoot his own crewman, but Louis Hendrickson cried, "Oh, hide me, Captain, hide me!" Then, before Clarke could answer, or even try to shout any sense into him, he ran into the bathroom and locked the door.   Looking around frantically, the seaman spied a little window that overlooked the quarterdeck, and he peered out — to see the two Malays murder the helmsman, who had stood numbly at his post at the wheel. Sobbing with terror, Hendrickson sank to the floor.

Up in the mizzen rigging, Sanborn was watching the same ghastly sight. "I then saw them kill Molony at the wheel," he told the reporters later; "who showed no resistance, but begged hard for his life." Terrified that the Malays would look up and see where he was perched, Sanborn swung along stays until he was in the fore rigging, and then dropped down onto the bows.   His muddled intention was to join his shipmates in the forecastle, but the door was not just barred, but tied with rope, so he took to the rigging again — just in time to see another murder, this time of the man who had been on lookout, and who was now hiding in the carpenter's shop.

"I saw the mutineers drag a seaman named Antonio Serrian from the carpenter's shop, and murder him near the main hatch and throw him overboard," he told the newspaper. Antonio, who had been one of those who had befriended the Malays when they had joined the crew, "begged hard for his life," but to no effect.

Having disposed of his body, the two Malays then "went into the carpenter's shop and sharpened two axes."

Once armed with these, one native went aft, to stand over the companionway there, while the other stood guard at the forecastle door. This was interrupted when Captain Clarke and Mary Ellen started firing at the one who was on the afterdeck, having reached the skylight by clambering onto the table. Dropping their axes, the Malays "got knives fastened to long sticks, and tried to wound the inmates of the cabin" by poking down through the skylight.

Dropping down from the table, Robert Clarke ran to the two little side windows, and smashed them in. He fired two shots, wounding one man in the foot, but then he collapsed with the shock of his wounds. He was on the point of death, with only his wife to tend to him, and the ship was completely in the hands of the two mutineers.

Clarke lay comatose for hours, until well after dawn had arrived. In the forecastle, the atmosphere was as fraught as Mary Ellen's state of mind in the cabin, aft. To make matters even worse in the forecastle, the mate finally died of his terrible wounds, watched with horror by eleven stunned seamen, four of whom were badly hurt themselves.

With daylight the natives finally noticed Robert Sanborn, in the rigging. They shouted repeatedly at him to come down — they "promised not to harm me," he said, "but I knew it would be instant death, so remained where I was." Robert had no way of defending himself, as he left his knife in the forecastle when he had come on duty, but now he managed to detach a block, and tie it to a short length of rope, "as a weapon for self defence." Below him, the Malays dragged the Chinese cook from the coal locker where he had hidden, and forced him to cook them some breakfast — "coffee, rice, fowls, etc." — producing savory aromas that must have drifted into the forecastle, where the hungry seamen were trapped.

And so the terrible day dragged on, while Sanborn clung to his post in the rigging. About midday, the Malays broke open the dead carpenter's chest, and arrayed themselves in his best clothes. As they strutted, however, Sanborn noticed that one of them was limping badly from the wound in his foot. An hour or so later, about five in the afternoon, they turned their attention back to Sanborn, much to his horror. "I felt a slight shake in the rigging, and on looking below saw a mutineer with a fiendish glare raising his arm to strike a blow upwards at me. I moved at once out of range of the blow, and struck him with the block I had ready." The Malay flinched and retreated, but Sanborn, taking no chances, climbed even higher, into the royal rigging.

As he observed with foreboding, the mutineers were just waiting for darkness to make another attack on the after cabin. With dusk, however, Captain Clarke was up and about again, much to Mary Ellen's relief. Hammering on the door of the bathroom, he persuaded Hendrickson to come out and behave like a proper man. As the *New York Times* reporter wrote, "He had two revolvers and a horse pistol. He took a revolver himself and gave the pistol to Hendrickson. Then he handed the other revolver to his wife. 'Leave two shots in that,' he said to her, 'and if I am killed you give one of them to our child and put the other to yourself.'"

And throughout the long night that followed, he, Mary Ellen and Hendrickson fended off the two Malays by shooting at them from the skylight and little side windows, while Sanborn watched from his fragile, swaying perch high above. Then, at last, another daylight came. It was Sunday. Sanborn had been in the rigging for more than twenty-four hours. Captain Clarke had been conscious for twelve, but still he managed to keep up the potshots at the mutineers, with Mary Ellen and Hendrickson at his side.

The two Malays, highly frustrated at this unstoppable defense from the cabin, set to tearing down the doors of the carpenter's shop, to make them into shields to protect them from the shots being fired. Then, with a shield in one hand, and a long knife-headed stick in the other, they approached the after deck for another assault — and Sanborn saw the cook creep out of the galley. The Chinese man was holding one of the axes, which he stealthily handed through the tiny forecastle window. Emboldened, Sanborn swung down from the rigging, grabbed the other ax, and ran to the forecastle door, shouting at the men inside. Then he smashed at the outside of the forecastle door, at the same time listening to the seamen breaking it down from within.

Seeing what was happening, the Malays swung around, dropped their shields, and ran forward. Grabbing a heavy bit of iron as a weapon as he went, Sanborn scuttled back up the mast and made his way forward through the rigging, shouting down to the captain that now was the time to break out of the cabin. Inside, urged on by the captain and his wife, Louis Hendrickson jumped onto the cabin table, and heaved themselves up through the skylight. Then he ran to the after companionway door, yelling as he went, and no sooner had he released it, than Captain Clarke came charging out. And, at that very same moment, the forecastle door burst open, and the seamen came out in a rush. "So we were all on deck at once," said Sanborn to the reporter.

Both Hendrickson and Captain Clarke had revolvers. Clarke was the first to fire, and was rewarded with the thump of a bullet hitting home. The Malay he had shot let out a terrible yell, and jumped overboard to his death. "The other villain jumped down the ventilating hatch," the *New York Times* reporter wrote. Clarke and the freed seamen chased after him — but then stopped short as smoke came pouring up from the hold. At some time during the long siege the Malays had prepared a fire in the hemp cargo, and now the second mutineer had set it alight. "In a moment he appeared springing out of the smoke. Then he glared wildly about him, and, giving a fiendish yell, ran to the side and plunged overboard."

The ship had been retaken — but the ship was doomed.

Under Clarke's direction, the surviving seamen hauled out the hoses and poured water down the hold, but the only result was a greater billowing of smoke. "We worked for four hours with no success, the fire gaining all the time," said Sanborn. Soon the deck planks were getting hot — then were too hot to stand on — then were beginning to char and crumble. The only recourse was to get out the ship's boats, and escape the oncoming inferno.

There were two boats, but when they lowered the first one, it capsized, so they reduced to just one. "A small quantity of provisions were stowed in the largest boat," wrote the *New York Times* reporter, while the *News of the World* added the information that Captain Clarke collected his ship's papers, his chronometers, and navigation instruments. The wounded men were placed as comfortably possible in the bottom, and then Mary Ellen Clarke and her child got in, followed by the uninjured men. It was impossible to do anything about the bodies of the murdered first and second mates, so they were left on board.

Though the boat, with its seventeen souls crammed into its limited space, was cramped and uncomfortable, they lay by the burning ship until after dawn, while they watched the blaze work down to the waterline. It was ten thirty in the morning when, with a series of groans and cracks, the *Frank N. Thayer* sank beneath the waves. And it was then that the castaways put up their makeshift sail and steered for the island of St. Helena.

Because Captain Clarke had his charts and instruments, their course was unerring. The weather was fair, too. Otherwise, it was a nerve-wracking experience. Their only mast was cobbled from three oars lashed together, and their sail was sewn from blankets. Five of the men were badly wounded, and needed Mary Ellen's constant care, along with tending her husband. Luckily, as Mary Ellen Clarke observed later, their daughter, Carrie, was a very quiet and well-behaved little girl.

It took them six days to get to the island, so the boat did not beach at St. Helena until midnight on Sunday, January 10, when the port was silent and unaware. The United States consul, James MacKnight, was roused, and so in due course the wounded men were taken into hospital, and Captain Clarke, Mary Ellen and Carrie were taken into his home. Luckily, the island was a popular stopping place on the route between Europe and Asia, so the captain and his family were able to take passage on the New York-bound *Servia*, where they met the same sympathetic reception they had found in Jamestown, St. Helena.

During the passage, as the *New York Times* reported, "an entertainment in aid of Capt. Clarke and his family" was given. One of the passengers had a fine baritone voice, while another was a well-known lecturer, and others had similar talents. By the end of the affair sixty pounds had been raised — $300 in United States money, which was no small sum at the time, and undoubtedly most welcome.

"Capt. Clarke will go at once to some relatives on Long Island, where he will remain until he entirely recovers from his wounds," the report went on. Naturally, his gallant wife, "who stood by her wounded husband during the long and terrible hours they were imprisoned in the cabin of the *Thayer*," was going with him. He still needed a great deal of nursing, the reporter remarked — Captain Clarke, who was very much bandaged up about the head, got "very much excited" as he was relating the details — "His wife would try to quiet him by telling him that he would injure himself by giving way to his feelings."

And what did Mrs. Clarke have to say about her perilous voyage? Not much at all — "We reached St. Helena on Sunday after a sail of 700 miles without incident" — was all the reaction the reporter could get out of her. And would she go to sea again? "Of course," she said with a shrug. "What else is there to do?"

Fire on the ship *Frank N. Thayer*,
from *The New York World Telegram,* May 18, 1934

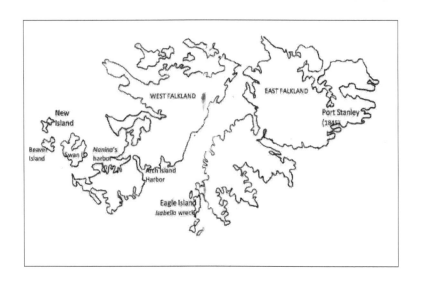

FALKLAND ISLANDS

View of the *Isabella* castaway camp, "Providence," from
Charles Barnard, *A Narrative of the Sufferings and Adventures...*

SEVEN
Joanna Durie

On December 4, 1812, the merchant brig *Isabella* weighed anchor from the penal colony of New South Wales, Australia, with a most peculiar complement of passengers on board. Joanna Ann Durie, the wife of Captain Robert Durie, a Scottish soldier who was taking his family back to Edinburgh on furlough, must have looked about the cabin table with a sense of foreboding and wonder.

One garrulous fellow was Joseph Holt, the so-called "General" who had surrendered during the 1798 Irish Rebellion, and had taken voluntary exile to New South Wales to avoid trial and sentencing. He was now going home to Ireland after a varied set of adventures in the settlement, some pleasant, others not so. Another Irishman was Sir Henry Hayes, a ne'er-do-well who had been transported after a notorious abduction of a Quaker heiress, with the idea of tricking her into a fake marriage. It was obvious within moments that Sir Henry and "General" Holt were deadly enemies, Hayes having been behind Holt's less pleasant experiences, one of which had been banishment to Norfolk

Island for a while.

Also at the table was a sea captain, Richard Brookes, who seemed civilized enough, but had an unpleasant reputation that he had found impossible to shake. He was notorious for having commanded a convict transport on a voyage that was one of the worst in the history of transportation — the *Atlas,* which, coincidentally, was the same ship that had carried Sir Henry Hayes to Sydney. Hayes had enjoyed a comfortable passage, as he had bribed Brookes handsomely. Not so the convicts, who died like the proverbial flies, as Brookes had taken so much speculative cargo on board that there was very little room for his official freight of felons. Not only were their crammed quarters filthy, as no one could get in there to clean them, but the captain had saved money on the rations he was supposed to supply, so the hapless prisoners were being starved, as well. When the ship finally arrived at Port Jackson, there were corpses lying dead and rotting in their shackles, and other convicts, hoisted out, died on the way to the hospital. Brookes had not been put on trial, and had evidently learned better ways, as the transports he had commanded since had delivered their convicts in reasonable health, but still people looked at him askance.

Another Scottish army officer was at the table. This was twenty-two year old Lieutenant Richard Lundin, who seemed formal and correct in manners. His behavior was suspect, however, because without any kind of polite delay he took one of the four female convicts on board as his mistress. These convicts were returning to England after working out their sentences — obviously, they had earned the money for their passage in the currency-poor settlement, but the question was, how? It looked very much as if they were ladies of the night, as people termed it then.

And, there was the captain of the *Isabella,* a man by the name of George Higton. He not only had a brooding way of muttering to himself, but was evidently overfond of the bottle. And he, like Lundin, immediately took one of the female ex-convicts, Mrs. Bindell by name, into his berth. A very suspect lot, indeed. Lurking in the background was a malignant stowaway, ex-navy man William Mattinson, who was running away to avoid huge debts, though no one, including Joanna, knew about his presence, yet. There is the added fact, too, that Joanna Durie was seven months pregnant. As future events proved, however, she was a lady who was fully capable of looking after herself.

Joanna had met her current husband, Captain Robert Durie, back in March, 1809, when his battalion paused at the Isle of Wight, on the way from Scotland to New South Wales. Joanna, whose maiden name had been Taylor, was the widow of a Lieutenant-Colonel Malcolm Nugent Ross, of the 71st Regiment of Foot, who had reportedly died in 1806. What attracted her to Durie is very hard to tell. The army, like the navy of the time, was a very snobbish service, and her dead husband had been a lieutenant-colonel, which was a much higher rank than that of lieutenant, which was all Robert Durie could boast at the time — and a purchased rank, at that. And New South Wales was a long way away, and had a very bad reputation, it being widely known that men were paid in ardent spirits there, rather than in money, so that drunken sprees were very common. And, while a decent lady like Joanna might have expected that soldiers were sent there to quell all this, it was commonly known that not only did the New South Wales corps countenance the trade in liquor, but they had cornered the market and were making fortunes out of it, which was why they were known as the Rum Corps.

But, despite all these drawbacks, Joanna Ann Taylor Ross agreed to wed Robert Durie, and a hurried ceremony was held on April 22, after what must have been a very swift courtship, unless they were old acquaintances. That Durie was considered a very weak and ineffectual man, while Joanna was considered to be as impressive as a tigress, is probably significant. While it is impossible to tell why she was so keen to sail away from England, there must have been some compelling reason, for that is exactly what she did, leaving behind the two children she had had with Lieutenant-Colonel Ross, presumably with relatives. But now, almost exactly two years after arriving in Sydney, she was due to return to Britain.

Captain Higton took the Great Circle route to Cape Horn, steering south of Tasmania (Van Diemen's Land, as it was known then), and almost as far south as the Antarctic convergence, flying east on the breast of the gales of latitude fifty south. A cluster of tiny sub-Antarctic islands lay in his path, notorious as the graveyard of ships, but he pressed on regardless. It was Campbell Island that almost spelled the demise of the *Isabella* — to everyone's surprise when they rushed onto deck at one in the morning in response to the panicked shouts of the seamen, it was to find that Richard Brookes had taken over command, because Higton did not seem capable.

With such a grim augury of the future, no one should really have been surprised when the ship ran ashore at Eagle Island in the Falklands, on February 14, 1813. Captain Higton had only just arrived on deck when the lookout shouted *Rocks to port!* — he having been snoring drunk in the arms of Mrs. Bindell. Another shout, this time of *Breakers to starboard!* — and then a tremendous crash and such a hard bump that everyone on board fell over.

"General" Joseph Holt's published memoir describes him sinking to his knees after picking himself up off the floor, and imploring Providence for a kindly intercession, while his wife Hester exclaimed, "Let us all, linked in each others' arms, go to our watery graves together!" This, however, has to be taken with a grain of salt. Not only was Holt's original memoir self-serving, with a lot of self-aggrandizing fabrications, but the man who edited it for publication in 1838,Thomas Crofton Croker, was a fairytale reteller who was fond of adapting stories for the edification of the pious and genteel. So, back in 1813, when these events were actually happening, it is much more likely that Holt was on deck helping sort out the chaos up there, instead of humbly down on his knees.

There, he would have found that Captain Brookes had taken over the command again, and had ordered the yards to be squared so that the ship could be run up on a beach. The ship's carpenter was stationed by the main mast backstay with an ax, and the instant the *Isabella* ground up onto the sand, he hacked it through with three mighty blows. The main mast fell with a groan, the far end settling on a rock, and making a bridge from the ship to the shore. The *Isabella* stilled. There was a fraught pause — and the marines and seamen lurched completely out of control, intent on raiding the liquor stores and getting sodden drunk. The only sane note was struck by young Lieutenant Lundin, who set to launching the ship's boat, with the unexpected assistance of the drunken stowaway, Mattinson. But no sooner was it being held ready for the women and children, than Mattinson and Sir Henry Hayes shoved to the front of the crowd, and with two of the other drunkards they commandeered the boat. Then, when they got to the beach, they abandoned it and headed off into the darkness, leaving all their fellow castaways stranded.

So it was a case of waiting for daylight, and for the tide to go down. It was now that Joanna Durie must have heartily rued the fact that she was heavily pregnant, a burden to herself as well as the others. However, with the aid of a bo'sun's chair, she was manoeuvered on shore, to be joined by her little girl, Agnes, and the other women. Being resourceful, she had the thought to carry a bottle of rum with her, so that when her husband and Joseph Holt found her presiding on a hillock where the other females were huddled, she was able to offer them a bracing tot of liquor. Being also very conscious of social niceties, Joanna politely apologized for the lack of fresh water to mix with the rum, no running stream having not been located as yet. But no one complained, certainly not the men.

After some polite small talk, where Mrs. Durie remarked that the rising sun was revealing country that reminded her much of Scotland, the men finished their rum and set to making a shelter. This was hastily contrived by propping some spars from the wreck between two hillocks, encompassing a hollow, and then draping canvas over them. Something better was needed soon, Joanna being so near her time, but in the meantime it was a case of rousing the soldiers and sailors from their drunken spree, and getting the castaway party organized. Captain Higton was obviously incapable of taking charge, so a council was appointed, composed of Durie, Brookes, Lundin and Holt. To save the face of their erstwhile shipmaster, Higton was also coopted, though reluctantly, along with his mate, George Davis.

And so, with the concocting of a set of rules, the camp fell under military-style rule. The castaways were divided into messes, each of which did their own cooking. Gangs were assembled to empty the wreck of everything edible, drinkable and useful, and the carpenter was set to building up the sides of the ship's boat, to make it seaworthy. The soldier who was the best shot was appointed "sportsman" and put in charge of killing off birds for the pot, and then the council turned to the thornier problem of storing the spirits and wine out of the way of the thirsty common men. It was no use putting it in a tent with a sentry on guard, because the sentry simply helped himself, and in the end it was buried, so that the casks could only be tapped with a hand-pump.

Joanna Durie must have watched all this masculine striding about and organizing each other with a growing sense of impatience. Time was passing, the baby was imminent, and she was still living under a sheet of canvas in a hollow between two dunes. When the sheet of canvas abruptly collapsed during dinner time, weighted down with water from the pouring rain, she gave vent to furious bout of weeping. The prospect of giving birth on a pitching ship in the South Atlantic had been bad enough, but now, because of that incompetent drunken sot, Higton, she was condemned to give birth on a plank in a muddy tent!

As Holt (through his editor) phrased it in his published memoir, "The poor lady was now near her time of lying-in, and had nothing but the cold and wet turf for the floor of her apartment. I endeavoured to comfort her, and told her that God had already been gracious, and saved all our lives, and was able, and would provide for her in her necessity." How Joanna received this pious platitude can only be guessed, but Holt, much more practically, then promised to build her a decent hut. "With His help, madam," he said, "I will have a house raised for you by this time on Tuesday next."

As this was Sunday, February 14, 1813, and Tuesday was only two days away, it's little wonder that Joanna simply stared, "as did her husband and Captain Brookes." However, Holt was as good as his word. Going out right away, he found a site with plenty of solid turf, which he (with probably a lot more help than he claimed he had) cut into sods — four-inch thick blocks of thickly rooted turf, each one measuring about one foot by two. The cleared area was raked and levelled, and then walled in with the sod bricks, which were stacked in staggered rows, each one with the grass side down. "At night I had the walls up of a cabin twenty feet long, ten wide, and seven high," he remembered. The sergeant of marines was requisitioned to go out to the wreck and fetch some spars and deck boards, and with these Holt framed the walls, and put up a ridge-pole, to which he nailed rafters. The timber was waterproofed with pitch, and then three good sails, also purloined from the wreck, were spread over the rafters to make a roof, "which, pegged strongly down, was secured from being blown off by the wind."

The cabin, now closed in except for a doorway, was floored with more deck planks, "and, having removed the stove from the ship, and cut a hole for the funnel, I brought coals out of the wreck, and one of the cabin tables, with a few chairs. By three o'clock," he went on lyrically, "the table-cloth was spread in the new habitation, and we sat down happily to dinner, and many a grateful bumper was drank, with thanks to me for what I had done."

Holt's timing was perfect — it was Tuesday. "Mrs. Durie, I am sure, would speak of me to this hour with gratitude," he smugly concluded.

That Joseph Holt was most probably exaggerating his accomplishment is evidenced by the fact that other huts were going up at the same time, each mess having their own shelter, resulting in a small village called Providence, complete with a provision store that was built over the liquor dump. While Holt could well have been the project manager, it is likely that he was just one of a large building party. And, naturally, his own house was a particularly fine one, with two bedrooms as well as an outdoor kitchen, which last he shared with the Duries.

Whatever the circumstances, Joanna's cabin was finished in good time, as she had five days to settle in before the first contractions started. Naturally, Holt had a great deal to say about the lying in, meditating that "my wife and myself felt very deeply for a lady in Mrs. Durie's uncomfortable state, and our feelings of pity and regret were much increased by the recollection, that a lady who had been reared with every tender care, and who had been accustomed to every attention, should be confined under a bank in a turf bog, without the comforts of house and home, and with no assistance but from God and Mrs. Holt."

Then, having braced himself with a glass of wine, Holt invited Captain Brookes out for a walk. Joanna Durie, being a lady with three confinements behind her, just got along with the job, with the result that Holt and Brookes were able to return just ninety minutes later to find her safely delivered of a girl. This was yet another occasion for a hearty bumper, as the two men "enjoyed ourselves proclaiming the young lady queen of the island, as the first-born there, and declaring her name to be *Ann Providence Durie.*" The baby certainly was the first to be born on the uninhabited island, and her second name was indeed Providence, but her name was in fact Eliza.

Meantime, the carpenter and his mates had finished building up the sides of the longboat, and giving her a deck, so Holt and Brookes walked out that very same day to enjoy another round of hearty toasts. "All hands went down to where the boat lay, and we launched her off the stocks; after all her stores were on board I brought down a bottle of rum to christen her, and you may be assured I filled my glass, and drank prosperity to *FAITH AND HOPE.*" The stores consisted of three months' worth of provisions, and she was commanded by Captain Brookes, who had a crew of five — George Davis, who had been the mate of the *Isabella,* Lieutenant Lundin, a marine by the name of Joseph Woolley, "Anthony the Irishman, as he could speak different languages," and an unnamed American.

"She hoisted her sails, and went to sea. We prayed for her success, as she was all the hope we had to get our lives safe off from these islands," wrote Holt. That success was perceived as being crucial. So dependent were they all on the outcome of the *Faith and Hope* venture that the mood about the village became more and more glum as the weeks went by and the longboat never returned. But then, on April 4, a vessel hove into sight. She was not the *Faith and Hope*, however, for she was bigger, sturdier, and was flying the American flag.

The visitor was a shallop, a small, sturdy vessel with a shallow draft and a single mast that was fore-and-aft rigged. As Holt soon learned, she was the tender of the sealing brig *Nanina*, which had sailed from New York in April 1812, with no less than five captains on the quarterdeck. These were Captain Valentine Barnard (the official commander of the *Nanina*) and his son, Chaptain Charles Barnard, both originally from Nantucket; Captain Edmund Fanning of Massachusetts (nephew of the famous Edmund Fanning of Stonington, Connecticut), Captain Andrew Hunter of Rhode Island, and Captain Barzillai Pease. originally from Martha's Vineyard. They were embarked on a commercial venture, to assess the potential of the seal rookeries of the south Atlantic. There had been quarrels on board, which was only to be expected with five captains all trying to exert their individual wills, but since arriving in the Falklands in September 1812, and building the shallop from pre-cut pieces in the hold, they had been doing pretty well. The prospects were so good, in fact, that the news of the outbreak of war between the United States and Britian had failed to deter them from carrying on.

While three captains were on board of the shallop, the one currently in command of the tender was Charles Barnard. As he recorded in his narrative later, the shallop was exploring the coast of Eagle Island, when the lookout drew attention to what looked like a flagstaff on a hillock in the middle. "We immediately repaired on deck," he wrote; "and in a few moments eight or ten persons were observed on the beach, and as many more were rapidly coming from the direction of the flag-staff towards the same place: among the latter party, to our great surprise, we noticed a female."

Reassuringly, in view of the fact that the Americans were worried about blundering into enemy Spaniards, Charles also saw some British uniforms — "I began to devise the most effectual means of aiding these unfortunates," he wrote, "whom I now onjectured to have belonged to some British man-of-war, which had been cast away on this desolate island." Their country and his might be at war, but as far as Charles Barnard was concerned, that made no difference — "as I felt assured that by rendering them this assistance I would bind them to me, by the strongest ties of gratitude."

This, at first, was accepted in the spirit in which it was intended. As Charles Barnard recorded, "Gen. Holt, (formerly of the Irish patriots) and Capt. Durie of the 73d regiment" came on board and spun a long tale "of their deplorable situation: that as winter was approaching, in that inhospitable climate, their only shelter was temporary huts, formed of pieces of wreck and sails; that they found no other means of subsistence, but what few provisions they had saved from the ship" — which, in view of the fact that the village sportsman had been steadily wiping out the island's bird life, and that sea elephants had been killed in great numbers for their edible tongues, was varnishing the truth with a vengeance.

Joseph Holt invited the three captains who were on board the shallop — Fanning, Hunter and Charles Barnard — to his house "at Newtown Providence, as I had called the little settlement." Then he ran to Joanna Durie to warn her to get ready for visitors. As usual, Joanna was up to the challenge, producing a well cooked meal, which she served out daintily, with decanters of wine and spirits to wash the feast down, all of which must have surprised the Americans, after the tale of privation that they had heard. She also chatted most entertainingly, regaling the captains with uncharitable anecdotes about her fellow castaways — "These outlines were generally given by Mrs. Durie with great spirit and humour," wrote Charles Barnard, who declined to quote her exact words, her comments being "too deeply shaded to rely on the honour of those described."

After spending the night in one of Holt's bedrooms, Charles explored the village. "The huts were erected on a high bluff, about a cable's length from the wreck; there were twelve or fourteen of these miserable shelters placed in the form of a square; the building, or larger hut, called by them the store-house, containing what provisions, wine, etc. they had saved from the ship, was placed in the centre. The sides of these tenements were constructed of dry tussock or bogs; the rafters of small spars or pieces of the wreck, and covered with sails or the skins of seals." Out of politeness, Barnard visited Captain Higton in his hut, where he found he approved of his *"chere amie,"* Mrs. Bindell. But then, after a short conversation in which Higton contributed only the words yes and no, the captain of the *Isabella* wreck pointedly reminded the American that breakfast should be awaiting him at Mrs. Durie's house. So, Charles, feeling undeservedly snubbed, took his leave.

Having eaten, Charles Barnard and the other Americans declared their intention to board the shallop, earnestly promising that the instant they got back to the *Nanina* they would let their shipmates know about the castaways and the wreck — at which point their hostess burst into tears. Joanna wanted to go too — "as she would prefer all the dangers and hardships she might encounter in our small vessel, to remaining on the island." With old Nantucket gallantry, Charles Barnard "offered to take her, with her family and all her efects, immediately on board the shallop, and though it was not my calculation to return so soon, yet we would bend our course of sealing towards the brig, in which she could remain until our departure, when we would convey them to the United States."

Holt wanted the same arrangement, but there simply was not enough room for his family and his servants. To soothe the Irishman's outrage, Charles Barnard said he would do his best to make up for it. Indeed, in view of the castaways' perilous situation, with winter coming on, perhaps the sealing voyage could be abandoned, and the *Nanina* come from the distant island where she was anchored to collect them all — despite the fact that their countries were at war. All he asked in recompense was salvage rights to the wreck of the *Isabella* — barring any private goods, of course.

That, the castaways all agreed, was very fair indeed — but were the United States and Britian really at war? Surely not! Charles assured them that it was indeed the case, and even made a formal announcement of the fact after the disbelieving population of the village had been lined up in ranks to listen. "The disclosure did not appear to make any alteration in the minds of the crew and passengers" — with the distinct exception of Sir Henry Hayes, who immediately proposed the seizure of the shallop as a prize, and then forcing the Americans to carry them to England. This was received by all the rest with utter contempt, as Charles Barnard noticed, and so he dismissed it from his mind.

Joanna Durie still insisted on sailing with the shallop, so Charles, as gallant as ever, instructed his crew to stockpile their seal skins on shore, to make room for the Durie luggage. Then he gave his cabin a quick tidy up, and handed it over to the Durie family. He even took on board one of the convict women, Lundin's mistress Mary Ann Spencer, to act as Joanna's servant, plus Mrs. Hughes, the marine drummer's wife, to help with the children. Then, after recruiting a few of the *Isabella*'s sailors to help with the *Nanina*, which needed re-rigging, he sailed, leaving Captains Fanning and Hunter on the island with a gang, to get on with salvaging what they could from the wreck.

Disastrously, on the way to the *Nanina* they picked up a small boat. It was the *Isabella*'s jolly boat, which had been recklessly taken to sea just days earlier, by the stowaway, Thomas Mattinson, with two boys and a marine. What would have happened to them if the shallop had not come by? When Mattinson was asked, he merely looked stupid, saying, "God only knows, but who are you, and what am I aboard of?" before going below and getting beastly drunk on the wine Charles Barnard had stowed for the Durie family. As Joanna Durie promptly told the American, when she came onto deck and found him, he had made a terrible mistake.

Mattinson's behavior confirmed the "debased and

brutal mind" that Joanna had described. Somehow, he contrived to be constantly intoxicated, to such an extent that Durie suggested putting him and his companions down in the jolly boat again. Barnard, who had overheard Mattinson wondering aloud how American prize money would drink, was inclined the same way, but Mattinson's three companions begged so hard not to be forced to sail with him again that Charles Barnard relented.

Barnard had more pressing things on his mind, as well. The wind and vicious weather were constantly against him, so that it was impossible to beat to the inlet where the *Nanina* was anchored. Finally, in desperation, he dropped anchor at Arch Island Harbor, on the opposite side of the island to where the brig *Nanina* lay at her anchors, and proposed that most of the complement should walk across the intervening land, leaving the shallop in the care of the Durie complement and one foremast hand. Then, after spending the night on the brig *Nanina* to explain the complicated situation to his father, Valentine Barnard, Charles trekked back to the shallop, with just one seaman as his companion. Then, with just two seamen — the one he had left behind with the Duries, and the man he had brought with him — and Durie and the drummer to help, Charles Barnard sailed the shallop about the island to the inlet where the *Nanina* was being hastily re-rigged. By all accounts it was a very pleasant excursion, with a walk on the beach and a demonstration in seal killing (though the ladies were squeamish about watching the skinning), and a couple of days shooting geese and wild pigs on Swan Island, enjoyed by all, Charles Barnard in particular, but it set a very unfortunate precedent for the future.

By mid-May, the brig was nearly ready, so the Barnards and Barzillai Pease had a meeting and decided to send the shallop to Eagle Island, with men to help with the salvage of the *Isabella* wreck. Because the American seamen knew the terrain, which the Englishmen did not, all the sealers save one went on the tender, leaving the *Nanina* with just five Americans on board, three of them captains, and one very old. To finish the work, twelve *Isabella* men remained behind, meaning that the Americans were badly outnumbered. And, disastrously, one of the Englishmen who remained behind was the brutish stowaway.

Not unexpectedly, it was Mattinson who first made trouble. Marching up to Barnard on the quarterdeck after Charles had spent three days trying to work the *Nanina* out of the inlet, he boasted that he could sail the brig himself, an act of mutiny that warranted summoning Captain Durie and having Mattinson put under arrest. Once the mutinous Englishman was confined in irons below, Charles finally managed to beat out to open sea — to meet even worse weather. The brig was blown back and forth, from one nerve-wracking bay or island to the next. Joanna Durie was violently seasick, and Barnard felt so sorry for her that he dropped anchor at New Island, and went ashore to dig potatoes from an old sealer's garden that he had seen there, for which she was properly grateful.

Once there, though, they were trapped. The weather remained awful, and so they had to remain at anchor, a long way from their objective. The three American captains and Captain Durie held a meeting, in which they "deemed it proper to remain on the island a few weeks, rather than encounter the risk of proceeding to sea in this tempestuous season." Accordingly, three anchors were dropped, the brig was snugged down, and everyone set their minds to the long wait for good weather. Then Charles Barnard decided to put the time to good use by taking a hunting party to Beaver Island, a few miles south, to collect provisions for the long voyage after all the castaways had been taken on board.

On May 11, he set out with four volunteers — one American seaman, and three sailors from the *Isabella*. And, as soon as their boat was out of sight, Thomas Mattinson led a party of armed marines to the quarterdeck, where he marched up to Valentine Barnard and demanded that the *Nanina* should be taken to sea, leaving Charles and his four men marooned. Valentine appealed to Captain Durie for law and order, but the British officer — who was supposed to be in charge of the marines — declined to put down this blatant mutiny, and so Mattinson and Durie's marines set to work with a will, briskly setting up the topmasts and the sails. On June 13 the weather moderated, and the anchors were weighed, much to the agitation of Captains Pease and Barnard — Valentine Barnard in particular, because his son and the four men with him had not made a reappearance. Finally, however, he agreed to pilot the brig to Eagle Island, but only on the condition that they called at Beaver Island for his son and his men.

Robert Durie's word was worthless. When they got abreast of the island, Mattinson simply ordered the crew to sail on, and when Valentine Barnard violently and desperately protested, Captain Durie and Joanna looked at each other, shrugged, and spread their hands. The *Nanina* kept on for Eagle Island, while Captains Barnard and Pease, with the one American seaman, tried to plot ways to retake the brig once they arrived there. Their relief when they saw their shallop beating out toward them must have been great — but no sooner had the brig's tender arrived alongside than it proved to be full of British navy sailors, who stormed the decks of the *Nanina*, bringing a British navy officer who formally claimed the brig as a prize of war.

And so Charles Barnard's fate was sealed. He and his four men were marooned on Beaver Island with few provisions, no wreck to ransack for building materials, and the icy southern winter coming on — the first of two grim winters, for he was not rescued from the ordeal until the day two English whaleships arrived, in November 1814.

For the background for this second act of treachery,

the story has to go back to February 21, 1813, the day that Joanna Durie's baby was born, and also the day that the built-up longboat, *Faith and Hope*, tacked away from the island.

According to the narrative of the open boat voyage that was written by Lieutenant Lundin, they first of all tacked about both West and East Falkland, hoping in vain to find a settlement. Finally giving that up as a bad job, they made up their minds to steer for the River Plate, which they successfully fetched on 26 March. At first the locals on the beach treated them badly, shoving them around and pilfering their few possessions, but then Lundin had the brainwave of donning his bright red uniform jacket, and the men who had been hassling them cringed away.

One of them ran off to fetch some soldiers, who arrived with an English-speaking officer. He explained that the castaways had blundered into the middle of a local war, and that he and his men were fighting the Royalist forces in Montevideo. Taken to the revolutionary camp, Lundin was introduced to the man in charge, General Rondiou, who not only offered to send the castaways into Montevideo under a flag of truce, but also imparted the interesting tidbit that there was a British frigate stationed in Buenos Aires.

This was a lot better prospect than being bandied about warring forces in a conflict the Englishmen knew nothing about, so it was back to the boat, and the passage to Buenos Aires. There, they met the lively assistance of Lieutenant William D'Aranda, who, despite his Spanish-sounding name, was the commander of His Majesty's gun-brig *Nancy*, which arrived the day after they got there. The brig had limped into port in a dismasted condition, having weathered a very nasty storm, but the British Navy lived up to its reputation for efficiency, and she was speedily repaired, manned and provisioned, and then sent out with Lieutenant Lundin as the pilot.

After a very stormy passage they arrived at Eagle Island on May 16, to find, as Lundin described, "most of the people absent, a shallop belonging to an American brig having approached the island in search of seal skins, and having given up every hope with respect to the safety of the boat, they entered into an agreement with them to carry them off the island; and all the able hands were now absent fitting the brig, which lay among some of the islands at some distance, to bring her round to carry them off."

Joseph Holt, who had been living "very merrily" with Captains Fanning and Hunter, was out walking with Andrew Hunter on the afternoon that the *Nancy* materialized in the bay. At first they both thought it was the *Nanina*, "but Captain Hunter, when he looked at her through his spy-glass, saw that she was an armed vessel." Matters deteriorated even further after Lieutenant D'Aranda stepped on shore, marched up to Hunter, and told him to consider himself a prisoner of war.

This took Holt considerably aback. As he said, "Here was an upside-down turn in the ministry, which put us all in a quandary, for much as I wished for a deliverance from Eagle Island, I regretted that any thing unfortunate should happen to those who had so well treated us, and who had acted in every respect like men and Christians." He was inclined to think badly of Lieutenant Lundin, who had not just piloted the gun-brig to the island, but had given him the details of these Americans who had done their best to save the castaways. "I could not help thinking this a hard case, considering their conduct to distressed British subjects."

Captain Hunter responded to his arrest with remarkable aplomb. "Very well," he said with a shrug. "Many a good man has been a prisoner." Joseph Holt recovered well too, inviting Laudin and D'Aranda to his house, where Hester Holt had a tea ready, and a decanter of wine was produced. Next day, Holt went on board the *Nancy*, to be puffed up with pride when he saw the crew all aloft, overhauling the rigging after the rough passage, a sight he mistook to be the manning of the yards that was the usual compliment to an admiral or a general. After that, feeling much more at home with the strange social situation, he was unmoved when the shallop returned, and the Americans who had been sent here to help with the salvage were arrested.

The *Nanina* was spied coming into the harbor in the early morning of June 15, to be met by the shallop and overrun by a British party. The British marines were most taken aback to find that the brig was already in British hands, but Lieutenant D'Aranda did not seem to think that Mattinson's act of piracy was reprehensible in the slightest — though there was some argument when Mattinson reckoned that he, not D'Aranda, was entitled to the prize money. Valentine Barnard and Barzillai Pease were duly arrested as prisoners of war, and then brought on shore to be housed with their fellow captains in Holt's house.

Despite the overcrowding, "I felt for them, with all my heart," said Holt; "and tried to make them as comfortable as I could, in their misfortune." He felt particularly sorry for Valentine Barnard, who lost his son as well as his ship — "I think that leaving these men on the island, was a disgrace to the British flag, and much worse in every respect than the seizure of the *Nanina*, considering the humane service on which she was employed," he wrote, but at the time he kept his mouth shut, it not being politic to express an opinion.

Joseph Holt and his family were assigned to the *Nancy* for the voyage to England, but he made sure of an opportunity to visit Joanna Durie on the *Nanina*. Their benefactors had been treated dismally, he found — "plundered of their feather-beds, which were ripped open, and the feathers let fly away with the wind, and boat sails made of the ticken." While it might have been a revelation to Holt that American sealers slept in such luxury, it was evident that they had put the feathers of the birds they had shot and eaten to good use — and, to an Irishman, who came from a country where a featherbed was considered an acceptable marriage dowry, this was a scandal. Worse still, the Americans had had their grog stopped, and their other rations halved, even though they were forced to work — "which I always thought was contrary to the treatment of prisoners of war, but the longer a man lives the more he learns."

What Joanna Durie did not tell him is that, as opportunistic and resourceful as ever, she had joined in the looting as soon as she had realized where the power in the camp now stood. As the American captains reported later, she rifled Charles Barnard's chest in the confusion after D'Aranda declared a prize of war, and then graciously presented the instruments to the British commander, in an endeavor to curry favor. Not knowing this, Holt then applied to D'Aranda to sail on the *Nanina* instead of the *Nancy*, and the English captain agreed, though very reluctantly. If Holt had done this because he thought the entertaining Mrs. Durie would be good company at the cabin table, he was gravely mistaken, and the Duries sailed on the *Nancy*, and Holt's companions were Lieutenant Lundin and Lundin's mistress, Mary Ann Spencer, who had already been on the brig a rather long time, as Joanna's servant. The American captains were on board as well, but they were forced to live in the hold.

The *Nanina* sailed on July 27, straight into a gale of wind — and it was then that Holt found that the brig was without nautical instruments, not even being equipped with a compass, because of Joanna's thievery. If it had not been for the pilotage of "that fine old fellow," Valentine Barnard, and the exertions of the American seamen, the brig would have been lost. As it was, it was a close-run thing. When the prize-master, Midshipman John Marsh, tried to enter the River Plate, as instructed by D'Aranda, the sealing brig was blown far out to sea, instead. When the storm subsided the brig was nearer Rio de Janeiro, so he steered for that port instead.

Rio was finally fetched on August 23, and once at anchor, the American captains came on deck. "I shook hands with them, and thanked them for all the service they had done me," said Holt, and then offered to carry letters on shore. This was gratefully accepted by the three captains, a development that proved to be very bad luck for D'Aranda, who was meantime steering the *Nancy*, with the Duries on board, to Montevideo. Letters were written to General Thomas Sumpter, the United States Minister of Plenipotentiary, and after Holt had given them to him, he consulted with the British Commander-in-Chief, Admiral Dixon. They both agreed that it was a very bad show, and Dixon vowed to do something about it. Accordingly, Admiral Dixon marched on board and released the sealing captains, who went on shore and sought out the American commercial agent, who witnessed their swearing of a formal protest that went all the way to the Department of State.

On the gun brig *Nancy* the Duries were having a very rough passage, but at least the brig made it to Montevideo, though with half the crew down with scurvy. There, Joanna and Robert and their two daughters took passage to Scotland, where they took up residence in Edinburgh. The little girl who had been born on Eagle Island was christened Eliza Providence Durie the following year, in February 1814, when she was just one year old. Months later, so tardily that there must be some unknown reason for it, Joanna and Robert Durie wrote a letter to the Admiralty, commending Lieutenant D'Aranda, "this meritorious officer to whose determined perseverance in surmounting every obstacle towards effecting our relief we are so much indebted."

By great coincidence, the Secretary of the Admiralty at the time was the same Mr. Croker who edited Joseph Holt's semi-literate memoir some years later. He already knew a great deal about the *Isabella* affair when the Duries' letter arrived, probably not just because he had read so many affidavits, but also because he had heard the story verbally from Holt himself, the "General" being one of his neighbors in Ireland. Curtly noting on the letter that "their Lordships have already been informed of Lieutenant D'Aranda's conduct," he set it aside.

People were to be informed of Robert Durie's conduct, too. It was November 1814, and Charles Barnard, one of the most famous castaways in history, was about to be rescued from the sub-Antarctic — free to publish his opinion of "the baseness, the treachery and barbarity of a Higton, a Durie, and his sentimental lady, who, to obtain her desires, was equally willing to call to her aid a tear, or a bayonet." Barnard was convinced that Robert Durie — whom he called "Sir Jerry" — was behind Mattinson's seizure of the brig, and the abandonment of the four men who were hunting on Beaver Island. He, Barnard claimed, was the ringleader — "Fourteen armed Royal marines had been placed under his command," but did he lift a finger to prevent the treachery? No, he did not.

But behind Durie was the malign influence of his wife — "This contemptible Sir Jerry had surrendered all his manliness to his lady wife, for safekeeping, for the sake of being occasionally warm at a dinner party or review," Charles wrote. "He had emasculated himself in feeling, and was a mere puppet that moved as she pulled the strings, so it was she that actually held the balance ... Madam Durie governed the automaton Durie, he the marines, and they the sailors and passengers." Perhaps, he went on bitterly, the British Government would applaud their action in countenancing both the seizure of the *Nanina* and the abandoning of the five men, and maybe even put up a monument in Westminster Abbey — "But I am perfectly willing that the infamy of their conduct shall be divided between the chicken-hearted Durie and his lion-hearted wife."

The future was to prove that Joanna Durie remained

as opportunistic as ever. When, she was widowed for the second time, in 1825, she had no hesitation in calling on the aid Prince Frederick, Duke of York, the Commander in Chief of the Army, by reminding him of her great ordeal on Eagle Island.

"On 10 February, 1813, our ship was wrecked on one of the uninhabited Falkland Islands in the Pacific and on 20th I was delivered of my eldest daughter which circumstances connected with our forlorn situation rendered my case the more extraordinary to compassion," she fluently wrote. And now, as she frankly admitted, she needed money — "Your Memorialist concludes in the hope that your Royal Highness will take her memorial into consideration and grant her with her four children such pension as your Royal Highness may think proper."

Whether she got her pension or not is lost to history, but that she was still willing "to call to her aid a tear" is yet another demonstration that "lion-hearted" Joanna Durie was as much a survivor as Charles Barnard himself.

Rose de Freycinet

EIGHT

Rose de Freycinet

Another woman who went through the ordeal of being wrecked at the Falkland Islands was 22-year-old Rose de Freycinet. But this castaway was a very different kettle of fish from the "lion-hearted" Joanna Durie.

Gentle young Rose was not even supposed to be there. Back on September 17, 1817, she had dressed up in a suit of blue frockcoat and trousers, and just after midnight she had sneaked on board the corvette *Uranie*. This was not because she was naturally daring, or a cross-dresser, but because she wanted to accompany her beloved husband, Captain Louis-Claude de Freycinet, on a discovery expedition to the Pacific.

Rose remained hidden in the captain's cabin until the vessel was well away from the French coast. Then her husband made her presence public, by inviting the officers, chaplain, and the expedition artist to a tea party where Rose, still in male attire, presided. According to her, it was a happy occasion. "I received them with a great deal of pleasure and I had a good laugh listening to the various hypotheses which each one had formulated about my identity." And the officers did not seem to mind, either, agreeing one and all that the dainty little lady with the charming manners and very agreeable appearance was a fit companion for her aristocratic husband — though some people said that during mess dinners the conversation about the dining table was more sharp-edged with brilliant wit than it might have been without a woman to impress.

When the news broke in France, reactions varied wildly. On October 4, the editor of the *Monitor Universel* declared, "this example of conjugal devotion deserves to be made public." Reportedly, Louis XVIII was amused. The Lieutenant-Governor of Gibraltar, the first official to receive visitors from *L'Uranie*, was not, and neither was the French Ministry of the Navy. Women were not supposed to travel in ships of the State, and yet Madame was there — in male clothing! It was unsupportable.

One result of this was that every now and then the artists of the expedition painted the same scene twice, one work being true to life, and the other *sans* Madame. This subterfuge was necessary for the official record, *Voyage autour du Monde ... exécuté sur les corvettes de S. M. L'Uranie et La Physicienne,* which was prepared by de Freycinet and published between 1827 and 1839. Madame herself was embarrassed that her presence was against the rules. She was not comfortable in men's clothing. The only time she was glad of it was when the corvette was pursued by an Algerian corsair. The prospect of being enslaved was bad enough, but "the thought of a seraglio evoked even more unpleasant images in my mind, and I hoped to escape that fate thanks to my male disguise." Luckily, the corsair veered off, after counting the corvette's cannon, and the possibility of the disguise being penetrated was averted. Then, after a disastrous meeting with the Governor of Gibraltar, it was decided that she should abandon male dress altogether, much to her relief.

But then, there was the crew. When Rose first arrived

on deck the men were deferential, leaving the lee side of the ship so she could walk in reasonable privacy. They did their best to refrain from swearing, too, but inevitably their self-imposed discipline lapsed, a curse slipped out, and Rose was forced to concentrate her troubled gaze on the water. This, once noticed, was considered a very good joke, and so from then on the men would swear and sing rude ditties just loud enough for her to hear, while the boatswain tried to shut them up by making violent signs behind her back.

In the end, Madame was forced to keep out of sight as much as possible. As the *Dictionnaire de Biographie Français* remarked afterwards, this was an admirable display of "moral superiority over the crew," but it did have the disadvantage that it made life on the rolling wave very boring — though Rose herself denied this, declaring she was happy enough with her guitar, her journal, and her sewing. She revealed herself more frankly when, on September 12, 1819, on departure from Oahu, she noted ruefully that "this part of the voyage will be greatly prolonged." Louis had made the decision "in order to collect data on the magnetic equator. However much I respect science, I am not fond of it," she complained; "nor am I likely to be reconciled to it by Louis' prolonging of the voyage, which holds nothing terribly exciting for me. It is true that this work is one of the main objectives," she allowed, but it was inescapably boring. "If only, like so many travelers, we were fortunate enough to discover some new island."

Louis had promised her that if they did find an unclaimed dot of land, he would name it after her. And lo, two months later, in latitude 14° 32' 42", they did indeed find an atoll that was so insignificant that it did not seem to have a name — and so Rose had her wish, even though she was not supposed to be there. "Let's see, what shall we call it?" the artist, Arago, mused in a letter to a friend, his tongue firmly in his cheek. "Let it be a flowery name. Shall it be Green Island, Red Island, or . . . No, I suppose it will be Rose

Island."

At other times, Rose was terrified to the point of biting her fingers until they bled. And yet, she never regretted her decision to defy custom and sail with her beloved husband. She had sailed to be with him, and to care for him when he was sick or weary, and no one could nurse him as she could! In ports (with the exception of Gibraltar) *La Jolie Commandante* — as the officers dubbed her — was an asset, too, for Madame was a marvelous ambassador, being most loyally French and a natural diplomat.

While her husband navigated his ship at sea and measured eclipses on shore, with equal *élan* she threaded her way through colonial jealousies and strange points of etiquette. When Rose decided not to attend a ball at Government House in Mauritius (because she did not think the expense of a new gown was worth it), she developed a migraine to avoid the social blunder being seen at a dinner party staged by her host that night. She was equally adept with native peoples. Rose was amused when the Caroline Islanders burst into roars of laughter every time the corvette's officers politely raised their hats to each other — "We must, indeed, appear as strange to the natives as they are to us" — and only a little taken aback when a woman in Guam, after complimenting her on her curly hair, offered to come on board and seek out her head lice.

Dietary customs fooled her completely, especially when Moslem guests left the table in horror after pork was served, but a Papuan pirate chief who "became very attached" to her chairs was immediately presented one. Another Papuan inhaled all the pepper on the table, ate all their pickles, and asked for "the plate, the glass and the bottle" he had used. These were gladly given (though she refused him the napkin), for Rose found him such excellent company. She even maintained her poise when some of the Hawaiian men startled her by throwing off all their clothes, layer by layer, as they got hotter and hotter while working their way through enormous meals.

Her descriptions provide a view of the early nineteenth century that is as feminine as it is French. There was, for instance, the celestial singing at a religious festival in Rio de Janeiro, in which the voices, "though far too sweet and melodious to belong to men, had a virile force and a vigor which were not characteristic of women's voices. I was overwhelmed," Madame declared, and took the first opportunity to ask details. "The answer" — that the singers were *castrati* — "conjured up a cruelty I could never have imagined before that day!" *Quelle horreur!* What a waste! More amusing were the native girls whom a party from *L'Uranie* surprised bathing in the Marianas, who screamed with embarrassment and flew to cover themselves, but were more concerned with veiling their backs than their breasts. "Methinks the gentlemen were not tempted to take issue with them on this matter!" And only a Frenchwoman, surely, would slyly remark, as Rose did, that a certain Australian was not just "very pretty," but had "a ravishing ankle, or so Louis noticed."

Departing from Sydney on Christmas Day, 1819, the corvette took the deep southern route around Campbell and Auckland Islands. She had developed a leak, but instead of stopping on the way, de Freycinet carried on. They saw their first iceberg on January 21, 1820, and land was sighted on 7 February — spiked with black rocks, and covered with short, dense shrubbery. The following day they rounded Cape Horn in mild, calm weather — "Was this really the notorious Cape?" she asked. As the ship steered north the weather deteriorated, and so they dropped anchor in the Straits of Le Maire. Then, while the naturalists were gathered at the rail, contemplating the lush vegetation and the thousands of birds, the order was shouted to cut the cable. The current was dragging the corvette onto the rocks.

Getting back to sea was no improvement, as the gale rose and tore at the rigging until the last sail was in shreds, making it almost impossible to steer. The ship lunged north for two stormswept days, until the Falklands were raised. Louis decided to head for French Bay (now called Uranie Bay) on the northeast coast of East Falkland Island, where repairs to the ship could be made. They were slowed up by a thick fog, but on February 14, the headlands surrounding the sheltered bay were sighted, and the corvette sailed toward them. All seemed calm and promising, but then they hit a rock.

As Rose described it, they were sitting at the table when the ship stopped in her wake a moment, and then sailed on. The shock was so slight that nothing was upset, but shortly afterward, water started rushing into the holds. The gentle blow was fatal, for a rock had pierced the hull. As Rose wrote, it was a dreadful, suspenseful moment — the bay where they had intended to anchor was still some distance away, and the coast around it was studded with sharp rocks. If only the ship could be kept afloat as far as a sandy beach, then the equipment and natural history collections could be saved before she foundered, so de Freycinet ordered the entire watch to man the pumps, while the others steered the ship and managed the sails.

The operation took ten arduous hours, and all the time Rose was abject with terror. She shut herself in her cabin, "overcome by the horror of our situation," and for a while she and the Abbé — the ship's chaplain — knelt together in prayer, but then she rallied to help the crew bring all the ship's biscuit to the poop, to save it being soaked. As the artist, Arago, put it, *la pauvre petite* "arranged it all with the minutest care." Every now and then she could be seen at her window, vainly searching the faces of passing sailors for a sign of hope. And all the time the men labored at the pump, shouting out crude, wild songs to keep up their strength and spirits. When Rose cried out that they must put their trust in the holy Virgin, Arago retorted, "In the holy pump, Madame!"

Whatever the focus of their prayers, it worked. At three in the morning faint, kind breeze wafted them up onto a sandy beach. The barren sandhills that dawn revealed did not look promising, but the company took the ship's altar ashore and said a *Te Deum*. Luckily, the expedition carried an abundance of tents, so that a village soon took shape on shore, though in the meantime the company still lived on the steeply canted ship. The next task was to discharge all the scientific material from the holds and cabins of the corvette, and stow it in tents according to order. Providentially, the weather stayed fine.

Four days later, though, the skies blackened, the gale rose, and it poured with rain. The beached ship was battered constantly, and settling further on her side, so that Rose had to go in and out of her deck cabin through a window, as the door was completely submerged. It was time to go on shore, and live in a tent. The canvas house had not been set up properly, however, and so the first night was a torment of being soaked in bed. When day dawned the first job was to secure the tent, but no matter how tightly it was secured the canvas leaked and their bedding was constantly damp — "We shall be most fortunate if we are not afflicted with rheumatism in our old age."

It was now that de Freycinet felt very thankful that he had shipped tradesmen in his crew, for he had the necessary carpenters, sailmakers, blacksmiths, and ropemakers to turn the ship's longboat into a seaworthy craft. They called the little vessel *L'Espérance* — Hope. Hunting and fishing parties were assembled to go foraging in the hinterland, to save as much preserved food as possible. However, fresh provisions soon became scarce. For the hunters to track down a wild horse was an occasion for joy, as otherwise their diet was limited to penguins or seal meat, roasted or stewed in water with biscuit crumbs for thickening. A wild snipe was a special treat.

Incredibly, the scientific work went on. With wonderful

single-mindedness, the scientists built an observatory, in preparation for an eclipse of the sun on 15 March. The naturalists determined which of the local wild herbs was safe to eat, and so Rose and the Abbé collected celery and purslane for salads to go with the horse meat that the hunting parties carried in. With joy, Rose found a sack of flour that the Abbé had intended to use to powder his hair, and so the cook was able to bake bread. Some essence of hops that had been procured in Port Jackson was also salvaged, and so Rose took up the role of expedition brewer, making beer by adding sugar. Then a box of 66 cheeses was found, making the occasion for a party. But, as Rose privately admitted, religion was her only real source of consolation.

On March 19, 1820, the sound of "extraordinary shouting" was the signal that a ship had been raised. Everyone rushed to the top of the sand dune that was closest to the sea, to see nothing at first, but then a sloop coming into the harbor. Three guns were fired, and a white flag raised, and in due course the sloop arrived — when, with French hospitality, the impoverished settlement offered the newcomers food and drink. "Imagine our joy at the thought that our exile would soon be over!" wrote Rose. However, they were to be gravely disappointed.

The sloop, it seemed, was the tender of a whaler-sealer that was anchored twenty leagues away. They had been hunting seals for the past eighteen months, and needed another ten months to fill their lading. Louis de Freycinet told them that he pay the captain well for passage to Rio, but the man in charge of the sloop refused to go back to the ship — he had been given orders to fish for eight days, and he dared not return until he had his catch. Showing him a document from the United States government that enjoined all American ship captains to render any assistance needed had a better effect; grudgingly, the sloop-captain agreed to go back, carrying an officer from the *Uranie* who would convey de Freycinet's message.

So off the sloop went, but in no great haste. Frustratingly, the longboat was now ready for voyage, but departure had to be postponed until the American captain's decision was known. Meantime, too, men were falling sick with colic and diarrhea, probably because they had been eating penguins. Getting desperate as the days dragged by with horrible weather and no news from the sealer, de Freycinet planned how to capture and commandeer the sealing vessel, while Rose agitated about the violence that this would involve. "May God preserve us and bring back the sloop bearing good news!"

A ship finally arrived on March 28 — but it was not the whaler-sealer. Instead, it was the 280-ton American merchantman *Mercury,* en route to the Pacific. According to the captain, a man named Galvin, she had struck a leak, and he had turned back for repairs. And would he carry them to Rio? Of course he would! But he would need help with fixing the leak first, if the French could assist? That was easy, too. Louis de Freycinet sent twelve of his best shipwrights on board.

When Rose learned the nature of the *Mercury*'s cargo, she should have become suspicious — it was cannons, for the Chilean rebellion. Which made matters somewhat inconvenient, as Captain Galvin mused aloud, as he revealed his actual mission. While it was possible for him to carry the French to Valparaiso, on the Pacific coast, Rio was out of the question, being an Atlantic port. Louis offered to pay enough money to cover that loss as well as expenses, but the master only agreed to think about it — though, as the shipwrights reported, Galvin needed help even more than they did, as the weight of the cannon in the hold was forcing the planks of the American ship apart. And, what's more, the Americans were short of food. Within days, the American captain was begging for rum, as well as the game that the French hunting parties were bringing in. On the other hand, he was able to give them some medicine.

Then, at last, the sloop arrived, with the news that the sealer-whaler was in the outer harbor. The whaler was the *General Knox* of Salem, and the captain, named Orne, was willing to carry them to Rio, probably because his voyage had been so poor. The problem was that his ship had been unrigged to make a clear platform for flensing the whales that the sloop brought in, and it would take time and labor to get it seaworthy again.

And, of course, Orne wanted money — 50,000 pieces of eight, or piastres. Arguing hard, Louis reduced it to 40,000 piastres, telling him at the same time that he had another offer, from the captain of the *Mercury*. Waving a casual hand, Orne declared he was glad of that, because he did not want to miss out on the whaling season, but nevertheless he kept on bargaining. At the same time, the captain of the *Mercury* was threatening to leave without them, ignoring the fact that the French shipwrights were still working on his ship.

And so the double blackmail from the two captains continued. Galvin swore he would sail next day unless some cable was sent on board; Captain Orne demanded permission to salvage whatever he liked from the wreck of the corvette, though de Freycinet staunchly refused, saying that it was the property of the French government, and Rose was perfectly sure that the crew of the *General Knox* would steal everything they could. Then Galvin agreed to take them to Buenos Aires — only half the distance they wanted to go — on the payment of 10,000 piastres. After another bout of argument, he grudgingly offered to take them to Rio de Janeiro for 15,000, but then abruptly changed his mind, asking eighteen thousand. "This is an enormous price to pay for the minor inconvenience we shall cause him. But he is a rogue who is trying to profit from our present predicament," she angrily wrote. Meantime, Rose packed boxes, and suffered from the wet and cold, scarcely able to walk because of the agony in her frozen feet.

Finally, after a great deal of insult and shouting, the company boarded the *Mercury*, two months to the day since the wreck of the corvette. "*Uranie! Poor Uranie!* You who were my abode for so long ... we must now forsake you for ever!" Rose's cabin on the discovery ship had been small enough, but here she was in a cubby hole with much of the scientific collection packed around her, lit only by a small round of glass in the deck overhead, which went abruptly dark every time someone stepped onto it. Worse still, all her painfully gained courage seemed to be flooding away — just three months ago, she kept on thinking, she was comfortably housed and very well fed, and the voyage was about to come to an end. But now she and Louis were in a tiny cramped room on a miserable foreign vessel, "eating indescribable food with strangers to whom one has to be pleasant and whom I would often like to send packing." Little wonder that she could not stop crying.

Fate, yet again, was ironic. The commander of the Scottish brig *Jane*, a 120-ton whaler that had been at anchor in Berkeley Sound (present day Port Stanley), just along the coast, arrived to declare that he would have been glad to rescue them all at no cost. This was Captain James Weddell, a man whose naval career had been interrupted by the end of the Napoleonic wars, and who went on to become a distinguished Antarctic explorer. He was delighted with the "extreme vivacity" of Madame, "who was young and very agreeable." Louis presented him with the longboat that the French seamen had worked so hard to turn into a seaworthy cutter, and Weddell christened her *Rose*.

Finally, on 27 April, the *Mercury* set sail, still rife with dissension. Galvin kept on altering his demands, while first the passengers and then the French company threatened to seize the ship. Finally, the dilemma was settled by buying the ship in the name of the French government, for the same amount of 18,000 piastres that had been bargained for the passage to Rio. "All this is preferable to coming to blows," sighed Rose.

The vacillating, blackmailing Galvin and his unpleasant passengers were set ashore at Montevideo, along with their traps, and the French company sailed on to Rio in their new possession, renamed *La Physicienne*. Here, Rose became reacquainted with friends made on the outward passage, listened again to the *castrati* (this time without a tremor), rejoined society, and refurbished her wardrobe.

La Physicienne was being repaired and refurbished too . It took over two months, but Brazil's gallant Minister of Marine would take no payment for it. They sailed from Rio at dawn on September 13, 1820. And finally, on November 13, three years and fifty-seven days since the night Rose de Freycinet had crept on board, the expedition anchored in Le Havre. It was a moment that Louis and Rose both welcomed and dreaded, for now they had to face the consequences of their actions.

Louis was court-martialed for the loss of his ship. The deliberations lasted exactly one hour and a half. Captain Louis-Claude de Saulces de Freycinet was completely exonerated of all blame, the court finding unanimously that he had done all that prudence and honor demanded. Rose's name was not mentioned, her presence being tactfully ignored. The ordeal seemed behind them. Rose, who had been pale, yellowish, and sunken-eyed, was once again able to dance all night, and Louis, who had been sick and racked with worry and pain, was back to noticing elegant ankles.

The voyage, however, was yet to take its tragic toll. In 1832, when Louis fell ill in a cholera epidemic, Rose was struck down while nursing him, dying within hours at the age of thirty-seven. Heartbroken, Louis survived for another ten years, but, as a friend remarked, it could not called "living," for he "only languished."

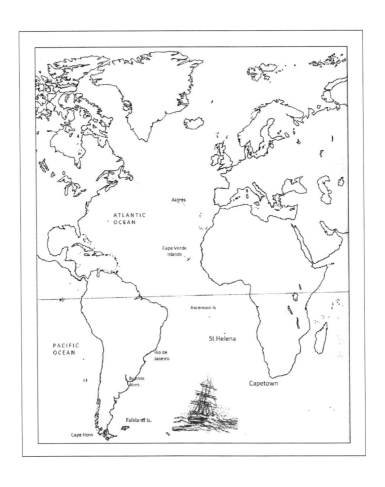

NINE

Millie Jenkins

The loss of a whaleship was featured all too often in nineteenth century newspapers. Not only were whalemen bound on voyages that might last many years, with the ship deteriorating all the time, but they followed the migration patterns of their prey into remote, uncharted corners of the ocean where reefs and shoals were lurking. Occasionally, too, the giant whale turned on its tormentor, and the famous *Essex* (which inspired the famous fictional *Pequod*) was by no means the only whaler to founder after being attacked by Leviathan.

"The most thrilling episode ever known in the history of the American Whale Fisheries has just occurred," reported *The New York Journal* in May 1902, under the headline RAMMED AND SUNK BY AN INFURIATED BULL WHALE. "It is full of the mystery and thrill and terror of the deep sea." To lend even more spice to the tale, the captain's wife had been on board! Naturally, then, the journalists lined up to interview the lady.

"Mrs Jenkins was not a green sailor on this voyage, for

she had been to sea before," wrote the New Bedford paper, and then explained that she was on the ship's crewlist — "enrolled on the ship's papers as assistant navigator. This is not a meaningless designation in her case," he went on, "for she is a valuable helper to her husband in taking sights and in calculating latitude and longitude." Not only was this useful for Captain Tom Jenkins, Millie's husband, but it kept Millie from being bored.

But was she ever frightened? Well, she admitted, she was not a fearless woman, and during storms she was often nervous. When the wind blew and the ship tossed she remembered "some of the remarks which my friends made before I sailed. One woman said that it was nice to be able to go with my husband, for if one goes down you will both go," while another had reckoned that it was a foolhardy thing to sail with him — Just think, she remarked, of being in mid ocean with nothing but a planks between you and eternity! — "This was not a very consoling thing to have ringing in my ears during a terrific gale," Millie laughed. But was she worried on that famous St. Patrick's Day when she was castaway in a boat? Not at all! She was as calm as the rest of the crew.

The incidents of that day were also described in remarkably matter of fact tones by her husband, Captain Tom Jenkins, in a speech he gave at a meeting of the New Bedford Board of Trade, which was published in a little monograph by Hutchinson and Co., printers of New Bedford, later that same year. "Having been requested to give an account of the sinking of the Bark *Kathleen* by a whale," he began, "I will do the best I can, though I think that those who have read the papers know as much or more about it than I do.

"We sailed from New Bedford the 22nd October, 1901, and with the exception of three weeks of the worst weather I have ever had on leaving home, everything went fairly well," he went on. Everything went fairly well, that is, until they arrived in the south Atlantic, abreast of the coast of Brazil. For a while, the prospects looked even better when they raised a very large whale, and Captain Jenkins ordered the helmsman to follow the whale's course. They steered in a zigzag as he breached and sounded here and there, losing him in a rain squall and then finding him (or his twin) again, in "one of the finest whaling days I have ever seen, smooth water and clear sky."

It was then that he had a happy premonition. As the lookouts were climbing to the lookout hoops at the top of the masts, Captain Jenkins told them to watch out sharp, because he knew in his bones that they were going to find that whale again. It was March 17, 1902.

Captain Jenkins was, of course, right — except that they found not just that one big whale, but a whole bunch of his companions, fluking and breaching and playing about in the sea. It was early in the afternoon, and the sea and weather were still good, so the captain ordered all four boats to be lowered.

Each one carried six men, with the harpooner — "boatsteerer" — in the bow, and a mate — "boatheader" — steering the boat from the back. The first mate, Mr. Nichols, was the first to strike. Lurching with shock and pain, the whale took off in one direction, while his fellows all fled in another, hotly chased by the other three boats. Captain Jenkins, watching from the top of the mainmast of the *Kathleen*, directed the helmsman to steer the ship in the first mate's direction, and by the time they came up to him, the whale was dead. And, in customary whaling fashion, Mr. Nichols had "waifed" the corpse — planted a flag in its back — and was sailing off in pursuit of the others. It was definitely going to be a good day, or so Captain Tom thought, because about three in the afternoon the lookout called out that the other three boats were all fast to whales.

Captain Jenkins had work of his own, concentrating on

the ticklish task of getting the ship alongside the waifed whale, ready for flensing — "cutting in" — the blubber from the corpse. Just as he was getting the job finished, though, the lookout called out that the only boat he could see was the one headed by Mr. Nichols — all the rest had sailed out of sight. "That worried me some," the captain remembered, and so he told the cooper to go on with securing the corpse, while he went aloft to have a look for himself.

And, sure enough, the only boat in sight was the first mate's boat, coming toward the ship. Mr. Nichols had decided that he had done enough for one day. Then, just as his boat had touched the side and he was about to clamber onto the deck, Captain Tom heard a whale spout — and when he looked, there was the giant whale they had been following for days. He was not more than five hundred feet off, swimming powerfully and fast, and headed directly for the ship.

This, Captain Tom Jenkins thought, was a fine chance to make sure of the prize they had pursued for so long. "Hey!" he called down to Mr. Nichols. "You get back in that boat and go after that fellow. It looks as if he wants to get aboard of us, so why don't you help him along?"

Mr. Nichols did his best to obey, it seems. He turned his boat around, and his crew rowed up to the whale, but the giant was moving too fast for the harpooner to take aim. And then he was so close that there was not room, the harpooner said, to get a good swing. Then, instead of veering off to windward as he sighted the ship, as everyone expected, the whale just kept on coming, faster and faster. Then, when he was about thirty feet away, he sounded a little as he kept on coming, which meant that when he rammed the ship, he was about five feet under the water.

"It shook the ship considerably when he struck her," the captain remembered; "then he tried to come up and he raised the stern up some two or three feet so when she came down her counters made a big splash. The whale came up on the other side of the ship and laid there and rolled, did not seem to know what to do. I asked the cooper if he thought the whale had hurt the ship any and he said he did not think so for he had not heard anything crack."

Mr. Nichols, in his boat, certainly didn't think anything was wrong, for he was all for having another go at the whale. Captain Jenkins thought otherwise — "I thought we had no business fooling with that whale any more that day as the other three boats were out of sight and fast to whales and night coming on." So he called out for him to come back.

"What for?" Mr. Nichols argued. The whale was lying there, apparently stunned, and the harpooner was keen to try his luck again. But Captain Jenkins insisted, so Mr. Nichols came on board, and joined Captain Tom at the top of the mast, so he could have a look for the lost boats, too. And then, just as he reckoned he had glimpsed the three of them, one of the men of his boat's crew, who had gone below to change his wet clothes, came tearing up from the forecastle yelling that the floor was covered with gushing water.

So the whale had done some damage, after all; in fact, the way the water was coming in, the ship must have quite a hole in her, or so Captain Jenkins deduced. He ordered flags to be set at all three mastheads as a signal for all the boats to return — but none of them paid any attention at all, their crews being so absorbed in chasing whales. If they had come, he reminisced, they would have been able to load bread and water and other provisions and gear in their boats, but it was no use, because they were intent on their whaling. Then it was too late. When they went into the hold to fetch a cask of bread, the cask floated away from them. It was time to abandon ship, so Captain Jenkins went down into the cabin.

Millie Jenkins was sitting on the transom sofa, absorbed in the book she was reading. "Hey," he said. "Didn't you feel that bump?"

"What bump?" said she.

"Never mind that," he said. "The ship is sinking."

As Captain Tom remembered it, he then told her to get some warm clothing, but that there wasn't enough time to save anything else. "Well," he told the Board of Trade, "the first thing she did was to go for the parrot and take him on deck. Then she got a jacket and an old shawl." According to her, the collection was in fact a shawl, two dress skirts and a golf cape, "and then," she said, "I saw Bingo, a fine gray parrot, which we had on board. I turned to ask my husband if I could take him along, but I saw he was too busy gathering charts and things. So I concluded to take him up on deck anyway, for if we had to leave him it would be just as well to leave him on deck as in the cabin."

It was now time to take to the boat — which had to be the first mate's boat, as it was the only one still with the ship. That it was there at all was fortunate, according to Millie, who told the reporter from *The Boston Globe*, "It was lucky for us that Mr. Nichols, the mate, was near the ship, for all the whaleboats, except two spare ones lashed overhead, were in the water at the time the *Kathleen* began to fill. It would have taken some time to loosen one of these and drop it overboard."

It also meant, however, the captain, his wife, the six-strong boat's crew, and all the rest of the men who had been on board, were crowded into a boat that was just twenty feet long — along with the parrot, because Millie could not bear to leave him behind. As she said sternly to the journalist from the *Globe*, "although a number of reporters have put words into Bingo's mouth, he did not utter a sound when he was taken off. He is a gentlemanly bird, and does not swear." And, in fact, he was too scared at the time to talk. Captain Tom Jenkins said nothing, either — as Millie found out later, "he thought when he saw Bingo in the boat is worse came to worse we could eat him."

"There were twenty-one of us in the boat," said Captain Tom, "and with the water and bread and some old clothes, she was pretty near the water, so deep that the water came over the centre board, so that some of us had to keep bailing all the time." Not five minutes later, the ship went down. As Millie remembered, "someone shouted, *There she goes!* and, turning, I saw the last of the *Kathleen*. She rolled down easily, until her sails and masts struck the water and there she remained with only the port side of her hull showing.

"Nobody knows how big a hole the whale made," she added, "but it was hardly more than 20 minutes before she filled with water and rolled over." The men did not stop to speculate. Instead, the priority was to get to the other boats, and share out the load they were carrying. Baling madly every moment, Mr. Nichols' boat's crew pulled like madmen at their oars, and at last they reached one of the other boats.

This was the one headed by a man named Manuel Viera, a boatheader who served as third mate. Viera and his crew were most surprised to hear that they had lost their ship. Once they had collected their wits, however, they shifted around to make room as, with seamanlike nimbleness, a few men hopped over from Mr. Nichols' boat to the other to lighten the load. Then night fell, but, as both Captain Jenkins and Millie calmly pointed out, it was a beautiful moonlight evening, so that they could keep on the hunt for the other two boats. At nine o'clock they found them, and they too, Tom Jenkins said, were astonished to learn that they no longer had a ship.

After sharing out the bread, water, and men, the four boats set off in the direction of Barbados, one thousand miles away, with ten in three of the boats, and nine men in the fourth. Captain Jenkins had given strict instructions to all three boat headers to follow in his wake, and it was a smooth calm night, so they had no excuse, but the next morning not a single one of the boats was in sight. He tacked about, and finally found the third mate's boat, but neither of the others, which at the time seemed a pity, because at nine in the morning he raised a large steamer.

They didn't even have to signal, as the ship was steaming directly for them. Then Captain Tom saw that they had a whaleboat in the davits, and realized that the steamer had picked up one of the two lost boats, and that the rescued men had told them to look for the others. Then the steamer came to a stop, and a rope ladder was lowered.

"We got alongside," Captain Jenkins recounted, "and she was way out of the water." He craned his neck to look up at the deck and then asked his wife, "Millie, don't you think that's too high for you to climb?"

"Tom," said she, "I could climb that side if it were twice as high." And she picked up her skirts and did so.

So Millie Jenkins's castaway experience was a mercifully brief one. The captain of the steamer — which turned out to be the Glasgow steamship *Borderer* — met them at the rail, and commiserated on the loss of their ship, and gave Millie and Tom his cabin for the passage to Pernambuco, where they took the steamer *Pydna* home. As they left the *Borderer* he even emptied his pockets and gave them the thirty dollars he had in American currency. "I must say that Capt. Dalton treated us splendidly," said Millie. Not only did he insist they take the money, but at the same time he confided that the only reason he had been sailing in the area was because he had taken a course eastward to try and get out of a head current.

Otherwise Millie might have been days in that twenty-foot boat, with nine companions, and just a small ration of bread and water. Nine days at least — for that was how long it took the fourth boat to reach Barbados, by which time the ten men in the boat had used up the five gallons of water Captain Jenkins had given them, along with the even smaller ration of ship's bread. As Millie reflected, she was a very lucky woman.

"We were very fortunate in coming out of this experience as well as we did," she said to the reporter. Indeed, everyone had been so kind and so very interested that she reckoned that if they could have hired a room "and put ourselves on exhibition we could have raised money enough to make up our losses, for we were looked upon by everybody as famous shipwrecked whalers."

And would Mrs. Jenkins go to sea again? Yes, of course. As the reporter noted, if Captain Tom Jenkins was ready to go on voyage again, "it is safe to say she is ready also."

TEN

Gertrude West

Another whaling captain's wife who had a close call —
though in a different fashion, and for a different reason —
was Gertrude West, wife of Captain Ellsworth Luce West of
Martha's Vineyard, Massachusetts. Like most Martha's
Vineyard boys, Ellsworth shipped out first at a very young
age, on the *James Arnold* when he was just eighteen.
Despite his youth he was very prudent, saving the money he
earned from his voyage, plus the incredible amount of $25
from selling the scrimshaw he had made.

In 1892 he came home from his latest voyage to find a
young schoolteacher boarding with his brother Clem. He and
this young lady, Gertrude Eager, became engaged, and when
he went off again, as the mate of the *California*, they made a
pact to read the same chapter of the Bible each night. The
following year, he was given command of the ship and the
agent, William Lewis, offered to pay all expenses for
Ellsworth to go east and get married; he even suggested that
he take her on the ship for a honeymoon voyage, and
Ellsworth went along with this kind offer, carrying Gertrude

as far as Honolulu before she left the ship, which was bound to the Arctic.

It was the start of a strange seafaring career for Gertrude Eager West, one that often did not go smoothly.

On the next voyage, again on the *California,* Ellsworth disobeyed the owner's instructions to leave her in San Francisco before going to the Arctic, because she had had a miscarriage, and he wanted to nurse her back to health. This lost him his captaincy. The command of the *California* was given to another man, and Ellsworth West went out as the first mate of the *Belvedere,* which was commanded by 56-year-old Captain Whitesides, who had recently married an eighteen-year-old salesgirl. Ellsworth and the new bride did not get on, and after a couple of open spats they were not on speaking terms. Whitesides, who doted on the girl, retaliated by handing over the responsibility of the ship to West, so that he could devote his whole attention to his wife. Ellsworth West was openly furious, and all the other captains and wives laughed about it, so it is probably no wonder that he was laid off. However, he and Gertrude did not waste the time, instead taking a course in navigation in San Francisco.

West was given the command of the *Horatio* in 1897. The ship had the reputation of being unlucky, but nevertheless Gertrude went along. She coped well, according to her diary, which consists of large, untidy notes. She always gave the position of the ship, along with recording what she washed and ironed and what books she read; she "sewed on" boat sails and dresses, made pillows, pants and napkins, played crib, painted bits of the ship, fed the pigs and hens, decorated the cabin with "deer's horns," and washed her dog Nancy. Being practical and modern-minded, she wore Bloomer dress, which was a knee-length tunic over baggy pants. She and her husband Ellsworth gammed (visited other ships) often, particularly with her favorites, Captain and Mrs. Montgomery of their old ship, *California.* She seems to have enjoyed her voyaging life on the whole, being happy in a matter-of-fact kind of way.

Then, in February 1898, the ship was battered by a severe typhoon. "The captain lashed me to a chair," she told a reporter in San Francisco later; "because the fury of the storm made it impossible to stand up anywhere." Then, after most of the sails were ripped away with their rigging, Ellsworth hurried down to the cabin to warn her to dress up in clothes ready to be castaway in. "I was so frightened my fingers were numb," she related, "but somehow I managed to put on four dresses over my bloomers. I knew without question that I was preparing for an open boat in that awful sea." That storm, however, moderated, and the *Horatio*, "though badly strained, weathered the gale."

It is probably little wonder that when Gertrude boarded the ship for another voyage, on December 14, 1898, she was nervous about it. She dreamed about the pets she carried — a yellow canary, a black kitten and a terrier: the ship was "metamorphosed into the bird, and the cat sat on a rock splashed by the sea. The cat's eyes seemed dilated and steadfast," she related, "and I knew that it was charming the bird and luring her to destruction. All at once the dog set up a bark ... then I heard the captain shouting, *Clear away the boats!*"

The dream terrified Gertrude so much that she woke her husband and sent him up to deck to make sure that everything was fine — and it was, but not so a little later, in January 1899, when the ship was near Kusaie, in the Caroline Islands, and all sail was set to get the ship safely into harbor before the first gusts of a threatened hurricane arrived. There was no pilot available, even if there had been time to find one, and so Ellsworth West was sailing blind.

Gertrude was in the transom cabin when her fox terrier, Nancy, set up a frantic barking, and ran up the stairs. Gertrude followed the dog, and when she was halfway up the companionway the ship struck on a rock. The shock was so heavy that she had to grab the handrail for balance. An instant later, she heard Ellsworth shouting, *"Clear away the boats!"* Like a flash, as she told a reporter later, she remembered her dream.

"Sound the pumps! Back all the yards and carry out an anchor!" the captain was yelling, while the bark thumped upon the reef with every foaming wave. It was obvious that the *Horatio* was about to break up and founder, so signals of distress were flown — "and though we were two miles from the shore the natives saw our predicament and boats were soon making out toward us."

With the trained skill of experienced whalemen, who were accustomed to lower boats in a hurry, the whaleboats were down, too. "I went ashore in the first boat," Gertrude remembered. She had been busy in the meantime, collecting her animals and packing trunks, and these, with the two chronometers, went with her. It was a nightmare scene, pitch-black except for the distress rockets that were firing. A native woman took Gertrude into her home, but she couldn't sleep, instead walking the beach, waiting and watching until the last boat had safely left the wreck.

Gertrude and Ellsworth were taken to San Francisco by the American bark *Ruth*, leaving one man behind. He took the chance to desert, most probably, or perhaps had been lost in the confusion. Twenty years later, he was still on Kusaie, living under the alias of "Captain Leander West," the name of a relative of Ellsworth's who had died back in 1870. "He has been paralyzed for nearly two years and unable to work but is being generously supported by the natives," ran the newspaper report, going on to say that the American geologist who found him, Professor W.H. Hobbs, had petitioned to the United States Government to have "Captain West" repatriated. Whether the State Department was equally fooled by the deception is unknown, but if Ellsworth had read the newspaper account, he must have been reminded of their very narrow escape.

"Shall I give up the life of the sea?" said Gertrude, at the end of the interview about the wreck of the *Horatio*. "Oh no. I am willing and ready to start on a voyage tomorrow, but for the peace of the crew I'll leave the black cat ashore. It so happened that the bark struck the sunken rock on a Friday" — considered by seamen to be an unlucky day — "and above the roar of the grinding wreck I heard the muttered imprecation, *Curse that cat!*"

So Gertrude indeed went back to sea — but not in the whaling trade. As far as Captain West was concerned, whaling was not just unlucky, but on its last legs as a profitable business, as well. So instead, he commanded ships carrying passengers, mail and freight from San Francisco to the Klondike Goldfields, and Gertrude went with him, as the ship's purser, until 1911, when they both returned to Martha's Vineyard to enjoy a well-earned retirement.

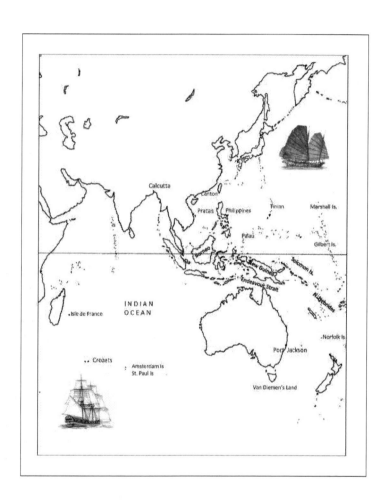

INDIAN
OCEAN

Calcutta

Canton

Pratas   Philippines

Palau

New Guinea

Endeavour Strait

Solomon Is.

Tinian

Marshall Is.

Gilbert Is.

Isle de France

Crozets

Amsterdam Is
St. Paul Is

Port Jackson

Van Diemen's Land

Norfolk Is

ELEVEN

Frances Wordsworth

It was common for whalers to rescue castaways, partly because they poked into remote, uncharted corners of the ocean, and also because they were systematically hunting the sea, instead of trying to make a record passage. A particularly dramatic example of this is the climax of the story of the English ship *Strathmore*, which on July 1, 1875, crashed onto a reef off one of the uninhabited Crozet Islands, in the southern Indian Ocean.

The *Strathmore* had left Gravesend, England, on April 19, 1875, with fifty passengers on board. It was her maiden voyage, and she was bound for New Zealand. One of the passengers was a Scottish widow, Frances Wordsworth of Edinburgh, who was traveling to New Zealand with her young adult son, Charles. The commander of the ship was Captain Charles MacDonald, a master mariner with a fine reputation.

The *Strathmore* took the Cape of Good Hope route, sailing south into the Indian Ocean. There was a ruckus about two weeks after sailing, when some of the seamen raided the spirits room, and drunkenness reigned in the forecastle, meaning that some of the passengers had to help work the ship. Also, Frances Wordsworth suffered badly from seasickness, and nothing she took seemed to help. At times she was so badly off that she despaired of living to reach New Zealand. Otherwise, the major problem was boredom.

On June 29, near the Crozet Islands off the Antarctic shelf, the ship was overtaken by a thick fog. The ship moved sluggishly, rolling heavily in the swell coming from unseen land. At midnight the first officer, Charles Tookey, took over the watch, assisted by the third mate, John Allen. The man in charge of the helm was William Husband, and ten seamen, including two of the boys, were on duty. Captain MacDonald came on deck twice, once at midnight, and again at two in the morning, to make sure that a sharp lookout was being kept. At three-thirty the lookout thought he glimpsed land, but was so unsure that he went to the forecastle to wake up a couple of friends to come and look. One of them, John Warren, heard breakers at once, and shouted out a warning, and the whole crew ran to the braces, hauling the yards around. But then, just as the sailmaker, Walter Smith, cried out, "She'll clear it, boys," the ship struck.

Panic reigned. First mate Tookey shouted orders for the boats to be cleared. The ship was sinking fast, and there was no time to fetch sails for the boats. In the cuddy, the frightened passengers surrounded the captain, who kept on brokenly repeating, "There's no hope — we are lost." The chief steward was frantically trying to collect provisions, but his assistant, David Wilson, screamed that there was no time to get them into the boats, that they all had save themselves. There had been no lifeboat drills, and no sooner was the starboard lifeboat full of passengers, mostly women, than it was found that it was jammed. Meantime, desperate passengers and crew were taking to the rigging, as the ship sank further into the sea. No sooner were they aloft than a great comber swept the deck, washing away all who were there, including the captain and the first mate.

The wave lifted the crowded starboard lifeboat, freeing it, but only to tip it overboard, upside-down, along with all its passengers. Frances Wordsworth was in the port lifeboat. Like the starboard boat, it was lifted free, but instead of tipping overboard, it rushed about the submerged deck, and then into the sea. When the grim morning dawned there were just forty-nine survivors from the original 87-strong complement, nineteen in the port boat, the rest in the rigging, one of these being the second mate, Thomas Peters. The only woman who had survived the nightmare was Frances Wordsworth, in the lifeboat.

The sight revealed by daylight was daunting in the extreme. They were off Grande Isle, uninhabited and precipitous, black with streaming rocks. Being able to see did mean, however, that it was possible for some of those in the rigging to venture down to the flooded deck, and launch the ship's gig and dinghy. Once the two boats were overboard, though, it was only possible to get into them by jumping down from the fore-yard. There was not room for them all, so sixteen had to be left behind, to wait with intense anxiety until the boats came back.

In Frances Wordsworth's lifeboat, the men had been baling frantically all night, to keep the craft afloat. Now, in the morning, their hands were swollen, chafed and sore. Now the gig, with Peters in charge, came up and threw a rope. It was a heavy load for the gig to tow, but Peters managed to get them to the bottom of the cliffs. High above, lines of seabirds roosted on guano-covered terraces, while thousands more birds whirled and screamed in the sky.

One of the more athletic men managed to scramble to the top, and let down a line. Frances, who was stiff with cold and weak from her constant seasickness, did not think she could make it to the top, but the men overrode her protests, and sent her up in a bowline. Shakily, she stood, and contemplated the bleak landscape. The island was so narrow that it was possible in places to see the other side. To both the east and west the ground sloped steeply upwards in pinnacles, becoming precipitous at each end, where the rock rose to make a mountain. A vile ammoniac stench of bird dung made the air almost too acrid to breathe. The only small comfort was that there was plenty of fresh water.

Peters, with three oarsmen, had taken the gig back out to the wreck. They managed to rescue five, who jumped into the sea to be picked up, but the rest had to be left to cling to the mizzen rigging until they could find a way to fend for themselves — which they did, by descending to the forecastle deck, where they lit a fire and toasted some ship's biscuits. On the way back to the landing place, the men in the gig picked up some cases of spirits that had floated away.

Meantime, there had been grave fears that Frances Wordsworth would die of frostbite and cold. Two albatrosses were easily clubbed down, and their warm, bloody skins were wrapped about her feet. Someone, too, had found her a pair of seaman's trousers and a reefer jacket. A makeshift shelter was contrived with canvas draped over oars at a hollow in the cliff by their landing place. When a plank was found it was given to Frances for a seat. More albatrosses were killed, skinned, and roasted over the fire that was lit, but only a few could eat the fishy, oily meat. Prayers were said, and then they all huddled under the canvas for the cold-wracked night.

In the morning, Peters took the gig back out to the wreck. Mercifully, the surf had subsided, so this time he was able to rescue the eleven men — two passengers and nine seamen — who had spent another night in the rigging. After he had taken them on board, along with the boxes of bread, clothes and matches they had managed to save, the gig was grossly overloaded, but he sensed that the ship would slip off the reef within hours, if not minutes. The sense of accomplishment in getting them safely to the island was diminished by the discovery that one of the passengers on shore had died. Grimly, Peters went back to the wreck, managing to pick up some timber, more cases of spirits, and some preserves to add to their meager store.

Once these were carried to the shelter, the three boats had to be left at the landing place, lashed together and tied to a projecting rock, because there was no beach where they could be hauled up and secured. With night came a gale, driving from the south with sleet and snow, and Peters sent two of the men down to the landing place, to make sure the boats did not break their mooring. In the morning the boats had floated off, out of reach. The two seamen had broached a cask of wine, and fallen into a sodden sleep while the storm had carried away their only means of salvation.

Even if they had been able to get out to the wreck to try to salvage more, it would have been useless, as only the tips of the topgallant masts now poked above the tempestuous sea. Grimly, the castaways turned to turning their tent into a proper shelter. Using planks that had floated ashore, turf, bird droppings, and rocks, they built up the three walls. The canvas, which was to form the roof once weighted with boulders, turned out to be not big enough, so it was a poor shelter, at best. Nevertheless, they called it Big Shanty, and covered the floor with cut grass, to make it as comfortable as possible. Higher up the same cliff, thirteen seamen built their own hut, which they called Black Jack's Shanty. Frances Wordsworth and Charles both lived in the Big Shanty, where the only salvaged mattress was reserved for her.

An inventory was made — two 25-pound kegs of gunpowder, a cask of port wine, two cases of rum, two of gin, and one of brandy, a case of pickles, eight tins of candy, a box of ladies' boots, two buckets, a hookpot, and a small amount of bedding, consisting of two blankets and some sheets. The confectionery was waterlogged and melting, so it was shared out at once, not just to give them strength, but so the tins could be used for boiling sea birds. After three days of near starvation, the castaways had no trouble eating the strong, fishy stew.

This set the pattern for the eight desperate months that followed, as the *Strathmore* castaways survived by making use of the birds that flocked on the bleak and inhospitable cliffs. Those men who were fit enough dug up mutton bird nests, first poking an albatross bone inside to make sure there was an inhabitant. These were white-headed petrels, which were good for food, being much more palatable than the other birds. Albatrosses were more easily clubbed to death, but their strongly flavored meat was hard to stomach. Their eggs were valued more, as they served two purposes — to eat, and to beat up into a kind of soap. They also hunted penguins, which were useful in several ways. Fat oily penguins made good fuel for their fires, while the skins of thin penguins made a kind of fabric, graded according to whether it was soft for clothes or strong for moccasins.

The coarse, oily diet gave them all diarrhea, and yet the castaways all craved fat. They were also acutely aware how utterly dependent they were on the birds. Knowing that the flocks had migratory patterns, they lived in constant apprehension that this only source of food and fuel would fly away. This became pressing in July, when the young albatrosses left their nests, returning only at dusk. The thrifty men, foreseeing this, had laid down stores of eggs and dried meat. Now the improvident stole them.

The castaways had learned to try to preserve themselves from scurvy by foraging for local herbs. There was a kind of grass they called "sea carrot," which could be eaten as a salad, while the pungent leaves of "Kerguelen cabbage" were added to stews. Nevertheless they were all suffering badly, with only about fifteen of the men fit enough to hunt. One good pair of sea boots had to be shared around, being worn by whoever was going out to fossick the terraces.

Many had very sore feet, while others had ulcers that refused to heal. One developed gangrene, from which he died in agony, much to the distress of the rest.

Quarrels arose, particularly with the Black Jack's Shanty set, as they reckoned that the Big Shanty people were cheating them. Curiously, a kind of currency had developed, this being the dressed tails of the birds that had been caught, the long feathers being particularly valued, and the men traded these for choice bits of food — or stole them while the hunters were away. Keeping order was impossible. While Peters, the second mate, had done very well, he was only twenty-three and no natural leader. Frances Wordsworth spoke kindly of him, and when he was unable to prevent the coarse swearing that offended Mrs. Wordsworth greatly, she was careful to say that she had been looked after as well as the appalling conditions allowed. Indeed, she had a kind word for everyone — one of the roughest was the sailmaker, Walter Smith, but she still considered him a "gem in his own way. He would knock down his enemy one minute and the next risk his life for him," she said; "and when he had a friendship it was to the death; he was always so generous and kind." It is significant, however, that she and her son soon moved into a separate little hut, where Charlie cooked her invalid dishes of birds' brains and offal minced up with sea carrot leaves.

Others also moved out of the Big Shanty, because there was so little room inside that the invalids had to sleep sitting up, with their backs against a peat wall. Because they slept so close together, too, they were all infested with body lice. Three of the passengers moved out first, building a small hut near Black Jack's Shanty, but of the three only one, Thomas Henderson, was fit enough to hunt. To everyone's shock, he was the next man to die, after experiencing a fit of insanity. The ground was frozen too hard to bury him, so the other two abandoned the hut, leaving the corpse inside it. With two other men, they moved into a fourth hut, which became known as Tommy's Shanty after the nickname of one of the builders. This was a much more elaborate affair than the first three shanties, having a floor of flat stones, and a stone chimney. To draw away the damp that had plagued the Big Shanty, a trench was dug around all sides. The men who lived there luxuriated in having enough room to stretch out to sleep, but they had to fetch their cooked food from the Big Shanty, an arduous trek during snowfall or a storm. Then Peters relented and gave them half a confectionery tin, so they could do their own cooking — though what they caught and cooked and ate was jealously eyed by the others.

Worst of all, perhaps, was the fact that at least two ships — the *Helen Denny* and the *White Eagle* — passed Grande Isle without acknowledging the castaways' signals. The first was raised on August 31, 1875. A hunting party glimpsed a sail from the heights where they were foraging, and two of them ran down to warn the others, while those who remained behind flew an oilskin on a stick. But, by the time all the fit men had arrived at the signal post, the ship was rapidly drawing away. This led to a great deal of bitterness, the man who had shouted out the news being upbraided for disturbing Mrs. Wordsworth and raising her hopes needlessly.

The second sighting was on the morning of 13 September. The hunters from Tommy's Shanty were out killing birds when to their astonishment they saw a full-rigged ship to the south of the island, running before the wind. Frustratingly, she was almost close enough for a man to swim out to her — if he had had the strength, and if she had not been under full sail and moving so fast. As the hunting party ran along the edge of the cliff, waving their coats in a vain effort to get the attention of the people on board, they could pick out details such as sails and spars. Then a thick snow squall arrived, and no more was seen of the ship.

Luckily, the severe disappointment was moderated by

the fact that the birds were nesting again. This, as everyone knew, was only going to be temporary — and, sure enough, in August the fledgling petrels joined their parents' migration away. Other kinds of birds arrived, and though they were easily caught at first, they soon learned to be wary of men.

As the squabbling for food and space became obsessive, men began to go mad. Some raved about rashers of bacon and hot mugs of tea, which would drive the others to their own bouts of insane craving. There were even fights over the flags that the castaways made and flew over their huts. One of the passengers, Robert Wilson, was attacked because it became known that he was keeping a diary, and the seamen who had got into trouble for stealing spirits early in the voyage were afraid that he had written their names in it. This led to the situation where some men were frightened to do lookout duty without a strong and trustworthy companion, while others quarreled over the daily job of fetching salt water for cooking, going out on the rocks at the landing place being so dangerous. They also fought over clothes, as everyone hated wearing the stinking suits made from penguin skin.

To break the tension, the castaways had made a habit of telling each other their dreams — "served up to breakfast like the newspaper," as described by Robert Wilson in his journal. Most of the dreams were about rescue: "many and varied were the yarns of safe arrival home, happy greetings and all that sort of thing." However, every now and then, "a vision more marvelous than ordinary" was related. One of the survivors, for instance, dreaming about Mrs. Wordsworth's daughter at home and was able to describe her with weird accuracy, despite the fact that Frances Wordsworth had never given the dreamer any idea of what her daughter was like in manner or appearance.

Frances had an uncanny dream of her own, in which she saw what she called a "white lady," a young woman she described in detail, down to separate items of dress. Then, on 21 January 1876, a sail was raised — and, to their boundless joy, that ship did respond to their signals. She sailed within a half-mile of the landing place, then came to and raised a flag — the Stars and Stripes. The vessel was a whaler, the *Young Phoenix* of New Bedford, skippered by David L. Gifford, who had his wife, Eleanor, with him. Their cruise had been very unlucky so far, and Captain Gifford had thirty men on board that he had rescued from a derelict ship, but nonetheless he lowered two boats for the castaways.

Mrs. Wordsworth was one of the first to be taken on board. And when she arrived on deck she came face to face with the "white lady" of her dream — a tall, slender woman in a fresh cotton grown, a kerchief bound about her head, and tied under her chin. She had the same pale skin and the same dark, lambent eyes as the woman Frances had dreamed about, and she was the captain's wife, Eleanor Gifford.

The men, naturally, were worried that Captain Gifford would be selective about who he rescued, favoring the passengers who had had first class cabins. But they muttered without reason, for all thirty-eight surviving castaways were welcomed on board the *Young Phoenix*. Hot water was boiled in the galley, and they took turns to wash, before donning the clean boots and dungarees that the whalemen found for them. Then the *Young Phoenix* sailed away from Grande Isle, while David Gifford debated with himself about what to do with them all.

There were sealers' huts on another of the Crozets, Hog Island, but the castaway seamen flatly refused to contemplate the idea of being put ashore there to wait until another ship arrived. Accordingly, he decided to steer for Mauritius, which was on a well-frequented sailing and steaming route. He guessed well — just four days later, the Liverpool ship *Sierra Morena* was raised and spoken, and the captain agreed to take a good number of the castaways to Point de Galle, in Ceylon. Then the ship *Childers* was raised, and that captain took Frances Wordsworth, Charlie, and the remaining twenty-two survivors to Rangoon, in Burma, and from there Frances and Charlie took passage to England. With Frances was all that she had saved from the wreck of the *Strathmore* — two rings and a rosary.

Captain David Gifford was warmly congratulated for the rescue — as the Board of Trade inquiry into the wreck concluded, "We cannot speak too highly of the noble and generous conduct of Mr. D. L. Gifford, the commander of the American whaler *Young Phoenix*, in giving up his voyage and rescuing the survivors, whom he appears to have treated with the greatest care and kindness." In recognition of the rescue, the New Zealand government gave him a gold watch, the Board of Trade in Mauritius gave him a silver claret jug, and the Humane Society of Dundee gave him a silver medal. Eleanor Gifford was not disregarded, being given a gold locket and a gold diamond ring at Mauritius. Even more touchingly, the first daughter born to Mrs. Wordsworth's son Charles was christened Eleanor Gifford Wordsworth, in a living memorial to the lifelong friendship that had sprung up between a lady castaway, and her beautiful rescuer.

TWELVE

Nancy Hopewell

There are many tales of daring at sea during times of war, but one of the earliest — and strangest — dates all the way back to July 1781, when British frigates were blockading the Atlantic coast of America. Daring Yankees ran the gauntlet, all of them taking terrible risks, and one of the most unlikely was Captain Elisha Hopewell of Salem.

Hopewell commanded his own small brig, *Mary Ann,* which sailed unarmed, because, as his wife Nancy pointed out, showing a frigate a clean pair of heels was the best defense. Arming the brig would be expensive as well as dangerous, and if they did happen, by some piece of amazing luck, to seize a British ship of war, there was no way they could take her over as a prize, not with their small crew of seven men.

Accordingly, the kind of cargo Captain Hopewell preferred was a run-of-the-mill one, like potatoes or sugar or coal, which was not likely to get him into trouble. Times became desperate as cargoes of that became more and more scarce, however, until one day he reported to Nancy that she would not be coming along next trip. And why not? Well, he told his indignant wife, it was just too dangerous. His mission, as he reluctantly admitted, was to deliver a hundred barrels of powder, along with a thousand pound of lead for musket balls, five barrels of flints, and two hundred muskets.

Then Nancy calmly asked him where he was bound with this cargo. Wilmington, North Carolina, he even more reluctantly replied, for this was running the blockade with a vengeance. But it was an important mission — the munitions were to be delivered to General Nathanael Greene, who had just achieved a strategic victory against General Cornwallis in an engagement called the Battle of Guilford Court House. While the Americans had been forced to withdraw, the British had taken heavy losses, and were licking their wounds. And now Greene, having retreated in good order, was preparing to attack the British at Eutaw Springs, to the south. He had an army of 2,000 men, and all that he needed was powder and ammunition.

"Powder," Captain Hopewell repeated, meaning gunpowder, which was notoriously unstable. It was a cargo that involved dangers even greater than attack by a British frigate, and a very good reason for Nancy to stay at home.

Nancy refused to listen. She had always sailed with her husband on the brig, and she saw no reason to change that habit. As the *Brooklyn Times* related, she "sent a few things down to the brig, shut up the stove, poured all the water out of the teakettle and appeared on board." Hopewell may have argued on, but if he did, it made no difference, because his wife was still on board at dawn, when the *Mary Ann* weighed anchor for sea.

Being the cautious type, Captain Hopewell struck a course that took them well out to sea and far beyond the blockading ships, before turning south. The wind held, the weather was fair, and the brig made good time toward Cape Hatteras. At last Elisha Hopewell, who was nervous by nature, began to relax. Then Nancy warned him that the wind was about to drop. Captain Hopewell protested that he was relying on getting about the Cape during the coming night, but Nancy shook her head. As a seasoned seafarer, she knew that her instincts were unerring. She had always been able to foretell a calm on voyages past, and she was sure of her prediction now.

In less than two hours the breeze died away, most inconveniently proving her right, and sending poor Captain Elisha's nerves to stretching point again. The *Mary Ann* rolled back and forth on the ground swell, and there were enemy frigates lurking on the other side of the horizon, the British being still firmly in control of the port of Charleston. Elisha greeted the fall of night with relief, though there was every possibility that dawn would rise to reveal the hulking shape of a British ship of war — but then Nancy arrived on deck with yet another warning. There was a big thunderstorm in the offing, she said.

"No!" he cried. "I don't believe it!" The seven-strong crew was equally appalled, knowing perfectly well that a single lightning strike could blow up the brig in a hail of splinters, but again Nancy insisted that she was certain of her prediction. "Get into your oilskins," she advised them all. "Because there is going to be a lot of rain."

The first flash of lightning came five minutes later, followed closely by a deafening rumble of thunder. Then came the rain, in a downpour that lasted over an hour. Throughout, the thunder pealed, each clap shuddering through the timbers of the brig like an earthquake. For the terrified captain and crew, it seemed endless, but the storm finally passed over without blowing up the brig, but also without leaving a breeze in its wake. Midnight came, and the *Mary Ann* rolled as heavily as ever in the oily calm that reigned. Then, just as Captain Hopewell was handing over the watch to the mate, Nancy arrived on deck with yet another nasty revelation.

"Can't you smell the whale?" she said.

"Whale? What whale?" roared her overwrought husband. "There ain't a whale within five miles of this brig!" At which the man at lookout in the bows called out, "Whale alongside of us, sir!"

And sure enough, there was a great whale lying nose to tail with the brig, rubbing his side against the planks, and blowing gently every now and then.

"What the hell are we going to do?" cried Captain Hopewell. Not only did he have just seven men on board, but the whale was exactly the same size as his ship.

"Nothing," said his wife. "There's nothing we can do but watch him until he decides to go away."

"But," he cried, "a single blow of his tail could stove in the side of us! Set off the powder!"

"Can't be helped," said she. "You can't argue with a whale, or tell him to leave, so you just have to wait until he goes, and hope he keeps his tail still. And I don't reckon anything bad will happen, Elisha. Fact is, I am more worried about our cat at home than I am about that whale."

So they waited, and though the hours slipped by, the whale hardly moved at all. When dawn brightened the tips of the waves, he was snuggled as cozily against the *Mary Ann* as he had been all through the night. Then, while the captain and the crew were lined up along the rail staring in fascination at their strange companion, Nancy arrived back on deck.

"Dear lord!" she exclaimed. "Ain't that a British frigate?" And when Captain Hopewell straightened with a jerk, she was pointing at the horizon, and there, sure enough, was a ship under all sail, flying the British ensign, and heading with purpose in their direction.

"We're done! Elisha cried, as over-strung as ever. "Go to the cabin, Nancy, and pack up your things, for we'll be in a

British prison before the day is out! The *Mary Ann* is as good as captured right this very minute! We'll never see Salem again!"

"Nonsense," said she. "That frigate will get becalmed, just the way that we are. He will have to lower a boat, and look, the wind is about to rise. It will whip up, and whip around, and carry us around the Cape before he even gets here."

"She's right, sir!" cried the mate, studying the sky.

"But look," said the captain, and when they all looked, it was to see that the frigate had come to, just five miles off, having lost the last of his breeze, and that he was lowering a boat with fifteen men inside. The crew of the *Mary Ann* could see the red uniforms, and the long oars dipping in and out.

"We're lost!" wailed the skipper again — but then the brig quivered, as the whale roused himself, and began to move away. He did not go far, just a few yards off, but they all saw him turn, just as if he was having a good long look at the frigate and the approaching boat. Then he arched his back, and down he went, flicking up his great flukes as he sounded, deep down into the sea. He had gone as mysteriously as he had come, and still the boat pulled toward them, until the crew could see the sun glittering on the bayonets of the marines inside.

Then, just as Captain Hopewell voiced another groan of despair, the mate let out an astonished shout. The whale had breached between the brig and the boat. He came up with a crash and a roar of spray, rising up into the air and then coming down with a crash. Everyone saw the boat hesitate, as all the oarsmen stared in horror, thinking the whale would rush them, but instead the whale kept on breaching and crashing, whirling the sea before the boat into a slather of foam that made even the *Mary Ann* dance.

"Have I gone squint-eyed," cried the mate, "or has that

boat given up and gone back?"

And indeed, the frigate's boat was retreating from the whale-created commotion in the sea. Then, while the captain and crew were all staring in amazement, Nancy said in her usual practical tones, "Shouldn't you set more sail, Captain, to catch that wind that is a-rising?"

The men jumped to with a will, and the *Mary Ann*, with all her canvas spread, had made a good two miles before the frigate felt the faintest puff. The English captain pursued the best he could, but the little brig had the legs on him, and by the time the *Mary Ann* rounded the Cape, he had given up and gone on his way.

"You saved the *Mary Ann*!" cried Captain Hopewell to his wife, and gave her a smacking kiss. "You're a hero!"

"Absolute nonsense," said she. "It was the wind and it was the whale."

THIRTEEN

The Anonymous Heroine

The conflict between the northern and southern states of America also involved stirring experiences under sail, one of the most well-publicized being the recapture of the brig *J P Ellicott* by the wife of the mate.

On January 10, 1863, the 233-ton *J P Ellicott,* of Bucksport, Maine, was on passage to Cienfuegos, a port on the southern coast of Cuba, for a cargo of sugar, when a black-hulled schooner materialized on the horizon. The Ellicott's master, Captain Devereaux, watched cautiously as the schooner steered toward him, but she was flying the Union flag, so he made no attempt to escape. Then, with paralyzing suddenness, the schooner ran out three guns and fired a shot across his bows, while at the very same instant that the Union flag was replaced by the Confederate banner.

This was the Confederate schooner *Retribution,* a vessel with a history as colorful as that of her master, who was sailing under an alias, and carrying false papers. Until the outbreak of the Civil War, she had been operating as a steam tug on Lake Erie, under the name of *Uncle Ben.*

Requisitioned by the Federal government, she had been brought onto the Atlantic seaboard to assist with the relief of Port Sumter, but after she was driven into Cape Fear River by a storm, she had been captured by the Confederates. For a while her future had seemed ignominious, as her engine was removed and transferred to the ironclad *North Carolina,* but then she had been re-rigged, and given a new identity as a privateer.

The man who had bought her, Thomas Power, had been issued with a letter of marque, giving him the license to chase and seize Union shipping, but there is no record of him actually engaging in the trade. The man who boarded the *J P Ellicott* was not Power himself, but a man who was using his name. This was Vernon Guyon Locke, a smiling, urbane, plausible scoundrel from Nova Scotia, who had allied himself with the Southern States. Without a tremor, he produced the letter of marque he had taken at the same time as he had taken over the schooner, in order to prove that he, "Thomas B. Power," was operating under license, and then, having established his dubious legality, Locke ordered that Captain Devereaux, along with his wife, his mate, and his seamen, should be taken off the *J P Ellicott*, and sent on board the *Retribution.*

The mate's wife was a different matter, however. Calculating that she could make herself useful as a cook and general servant, Locke decided that she should stay on board to look after his prize crew. This consisted of Gilbert Hay, a Scotchman, who was the prize master, another fellow, by the name of John Gilbert, who was to act as Hay's mate, and five black seamen from the Danish-held island of St. Thomas. Once they were on board and had been given orders to take in all sail and lay to for the night, Locke departed for his schooner, telling Hay that he would return with more instructions in the morning.

Left alone with the prize crew, the mate's wife eyed them warily, summing them up with years of sailing the

Atlantic behind her. The five black seamen looked innocent enough, but Hay was a seasoned rogue who boasted of having commanded a privateer of his own until it was seized and he was thrown into prison, while Gilbert had deserted from the brig *Gilmore Meredith,* where he had been second mate. Further, as she soon found, they had both joined Locke readily, enticed by the advance of $25 that he paid them, and the promises he had made of a great deal more as the prizes were taken and their cargoes were illegally sold off in the British-held Bahamas.

As soon as Locke had gone, Hay and Gilbert headed down to the cabin, leaving the seamen to take care of the brig. After all, it was going nowhere, and there was nothing much to do. Silently, the mate's wife cooked them a meal and served it, along with two generous beakers of grog to help wash it down. When this was eagerly swigged, she quietly put a couple of bottles on the table, too, convenient to their elbows for refilling at will.

When dawn broke, Gilbert and Hay were snoring drunk, heads down and senseless. The mate's wife went up on deck, looked about the sparkling sea, and to her delight and surprise the privateer schooner was nowhere in sight. Locke, she deduced, had decided to sail off in the night, doubtlessly on the hunt for more prizes.

She approached the two seamen on duty, found out that their names were Thomas Coin and John Wilson, and during a friendly chat she learned that they were reluctant recruits to the pirating business, having had no idea of Locke's plans before they left St. Thomas. Judging her moment, she showed them the handcuffs she had stolen out of a cupboard, and told them about the inebriated condition of their two officers. And so a plan to retake the *J P Ellicott* was hatched. The other three seamen agreed to join the conspiracy, and when Hay and Gilbert came to, it was to find that they were in shackles, and that the brig was under full sail again, creaming up the sea on the way to freedom.

None of the seamen knew how to navigate, but that was no problem, as the mate's wife had been taught how to chart a course. Assuming command, she steered for St. Thomas, speaking a French vessel on the way, where the captain confirmed her calculations. She was a little off-target, arriving at Tortola Island instead of her goal, but the locals sent a man on board to pilot her into harbor. And there, having safely anchored, she went on shore and reported to the United States Consul, John T. Edgar, who marched on board the brig in the formidable company of Captain Edward Nichols, commander of U. S. S. *Alabama*.

"SIR," wrote Captain Nichols to the Secretary of the Navy, in a report dated January 29, 1863.

"On the evening of January 18 an American brig appeared off the harbor of St. Thomas, and a report was sent in from her that she had been a prize to the Confederate privateer schooner *Retribution,* and had been recaptured by the prize crew. I immediately went on board of her in company with John T. Edgar, esq., U.S. consul, and finding the facts as above stated, placed an officer and four armed men in charge, with orders to lay off and on during the night.

"On the following morning the consul, ascertaining from the governor that no difficulty would be made by the Danish authorities, the brig was brought into port and placed in the hands of the consul, the prize crew of seven men being brought on board this vessel for safe-keeping. It appears from the deposition of some of these men that the arms, ammunition, etc., for the *Retribution* were transferred from that vessel in the harbor of St. Thomas to the schooner *Dixie*, which sailed in the night in violation of the port regulations, as stated in my letter of January 14. The two vessels met at the island of Blanquilla, in latitude 11° 52′ N., longitude 64° 41′ W., where the arms, etc., were retransferred to the *Retribution*, and the *Dixie* sailed, supposed for Turk's Island for salt, thence to a Southern port. The *Retribution* mounted her guns, one 20-pounder rifle and two smoothbore 12-pounders, refitted rigging, etc., and on the 3d of January appeared off. St. Thomas and chased two American vessels back to port.

"The next day she sailed north, and on the 10th fell in with and captured the American brig *J. P. Ellicott,* of Bucksport, Me., bound from Boston to Cienfuegos. A prize crew of five seamen and two officers was placed on board with orders to remain by the schooner during the night and they would receive definite orders in the morning. Gilbert Hay and Thomas Gilbert were in charge. The officers and crew of the *Ellicott* were taken on board the schooner and the wife of the mate left on board the brig. In the morning the schooner was not in sight, and the prize crew determined to recapture and carry the vessel to New York.

"The first part of this plan they accomplished under the lead of Thomas Coin and John Wilson, by placing Hay and Gilbert in irons, and headed the brig for New York, but the weather being heavy and the brig leaking badly, they bore up for St. Thomas, where they arrived as above stated. Hay is an old offender, having been captured while in command of the privateer *Beauregard*. Gilbert deserted from the American brig *Gilmore Meredith* (of which he was second mate) at St. Thomas. Coin and Wilson deserted from the same vessel at the same time and all joined the *Retribution*, receiving $25 advance and the promise of $50 more if successful in running the blockade inward.

"They deny any knowledge of the intention of the captain to go privateering until they were informed of it the day after leaving St. Thomas. Gilbert agreed to continue in her at $25 per month and two shares in prizes. Coin and Wilson, the two leading men in the recapture, deserve credit, and are entitled to some reward from the owners or insurers. I would respectfully recommend the five men composing the crew to the clemency of his Excellency the President of the United States," he concluded, having successfully avoided giving any credit to the mate's wife who had engineered the recapture.

Newspapers all about the northern states were not so neglectful, as the story of her feat appeared in column after column. Her name, however, was never given. Perhaps none of them knew it.

RonDruett

FOURTEEN

Lucretia Jansz

On October 29, 1628, a seven-strong fleet of East Indiamen sailed from the Texel, headed for the new Dutch post of Batavia, at the island of Java in the East Indies, on the far side of the world. The ships had been sheltering in the haven for two or three days, while their passengers vied for room to make themselves comfortable and the shipboard routine began to make itself felt, and now at last they had a fair wind. They made a grand sight as they paraded to sea, banners flying from masts and staffs, their multi-galleried sterns elaborately carved, painted and gilded, the carved red lion of Holland set at both the stern and the prow. Immense sails billowed, and slowly they left Amsterdam, the richest city in Europe at the time, in their wake.

Because of the threat of pirates and privateers, the fleet was convoyed by a ship of war, *Buren*. The six ships the *Buren* was coaxing into convoy order were the *Dordrecht*, *Gailliasse*, *Assendelft*, *Sardam*, *Cleenen Davidt* — and the *Batavia*, which at 600 tons was probably the largest. She also had two persons of importance to this story on board of this, her maiden voyage. One was a wealthy and beautiful young matron by the name of Lucretia Jansz, who was travelling to Batavia to join her husband, Boudewijn Van der Mijlen. And the other was Francisco Pelsaert, who was the boss of the fleet.

Pelsaert was not a mariner. Instead, he was an influential, experienced, and very well respected senior merchant. Ships in the Dutch East India Company were organized differently from their English equivalent, being much more like town councils. The top-ranked seaman was the Skipper, who was assisted by an Uppersteersman, or first mate, two or three Understeersmen (or second, third and fourth mates), and the High Boatswain. The skipper's only job was to sail the ship — he was not even responsible for shipboard discipline, as Dutch ships carried a provost, who did not just maintain the law, but kept time as well, striking the mainmast three times with a mace to signal the end of the watch. In effect, he was the shipboard equivalent of the watchman, or town crier, back in Amsterdam. Unlike the system in the English navy, where surgeons, their mates, and medical chests were sent on board by the Surgeon General, there was no man by the name of surgeon on board. Instead, the ship's barber had the job of trying to mend the hurt and ill. On the *Batavia* there was a chaplain, the Predikant, but on many ships there was just a sick-consoler, who did his best to make dying as comfortable as possible.

Daily matters, including the course and destination, were administered by a committee, and the chairman of this was always the most senior merchant on board. While the skipper was the navigator, and also a member of the committee, he was subject to the decisions of the other members. As a joint council, they issued sailing orders, adjudicated punishments, and sent reports back home. And the fleet as a whole was managed by another committee, known as the Broad Council. This was drawn from the merchants and skippers of all the ships, but again the chairman was never one of the mariners. Instead, one of the senior merchants was appointed Fleet President, and addressed as either President or Commandeur. And, in the case of this particular fleet, the Commandeur was Francisco Pelsaert.

Pelsaert's considerable administrative and diplomatic skills were taxed before the voyage even started. There was bad history between him and the skipper of the *Batavia*, Ariaen Jacobsz, a moody man who clung to grudges, and who was over-fond of the bottle. There was a distraction from open enmity while the fleet was scattered by a storm in the North Sea, but this worked to Jacobsz' advantage. When the weather moderated, the *Buren* had just two ships to convoy and protect, those being the *Batavia* and the *Assendelft*, which meant that the ship was out of reach of the Broad Council. So, Jacobsz, scenting his opportunity, set to making trouble for the man he hated.

Meantime, he had made blatant sexual advances to the beautiful Lucretia Jansz, which she haughtily spurned even after he tried to buy her favors with money and jewels, so that was another person on board who had earned his loathing. His passion was easily diverted to her much more cooperative maid, Zwaantie Hendrix, who, according to Pelsaert, "readily accepted the Caresses of the skipper with great willingness and refused him nothing, whatsoever he desired." Nonetheless, Jacobsz was still vindictive enough to wreak a vulgar kind of revenge by spreading rumors that Lucretia was a whore, along with plotting to involve her in Pelsaert's downfall.

The three ships made the Cape of Good Hope in good season, and Pelsaert managed to obtain meat from the natives on shore, but while they were there Jacobsz indulged in a drunken spree. Driven past patience, the Commandeur publicly and formally reprimanded the skipper — a bitter and humiliating insult, which was yet another reason for revenge. And what better means of having vengeance on the merchant, than by seizing the ship? All the skipper needed to do was deliberately sail out of sight of the *Buren* and *Assendelft*, and then, once the ship was alone in an empty sea, take over the *Batavia*, along with her passengers — including the scornful and beautiful Lucretia — and her rich cargo of silver.

But first, the vindictive skipper had to get the crew on his side. Jacobsz found a ready co-conspirator in the shape of Francisco Pelsaert's undermerchant, a thirty-year-old ex-apothecary from the town of Harlem, Jeronimus Cornelisz. According to Pelsaert's testimony later, when Cornelisz asked how the takeover the ship could be done Jacobsz replied that it would be easy — "I shall get most of the officers on my side and the principal sailors." And what about the soldiers who were being transported to man the garrison at Java? That was even easier, as the door to their shipboard barracks would be nailed up, keeping them trapped "until we are Masters."

Luck seemed to be on the conspirators' side, because Pelsaert succumbed to a bout of some malady he had picked up in India, which may have been malaria. For a while the barber gave him up for dead, and as he slowly recovered he was still very weak. And it was then that Cornelisz and Jacobsz put the first part of their plan into effect. The idea was to stage an attack on Lucretia that was so scandalous and shocking that Pelsaert would be forced to hand out very severe punishments, thus earning the enmity of the crew. Zwaantie, Lucretia's maid, was keen for Lucretia's cheeks to be slashed, ruining her beauty, but Jacobsz had a much better idea, which he shared with the very amused and willing High Boatswain.

Accordingly, a gang of masked seamen, urged on by Cornelisz and headed by the Boatswain, cornered Lucretia in her alcove at night, and stripped her. Then she was hauled on deck and hung by her heels over the rail, and while she screamed and struggled, terrified of being dropped into the sea, they smeared her with human excreta — something that was easily found on the ships of the time, because seamen who were too sick or lazy to go up to deck emptied their bowels in dark corners of the hold.

Naturally, once she was allowed to escape, Lucretia ran to the Commandeur, hysterically weeping, and obviously, he had to do something about it. As Pelsaert exclaimed later, it was a "gross evil and public assault." Jacobsz, who had taken care not to be involved in the assault, now publicly declared himself the defender of his innocent crew, while privately he was stirring up the seamen by telling them that the entire complement was to be punished — for something as trivial as having a little fun with a woman!

And so the road to rebellion was laid out.

The chosen date for the uprising was June 4, 1629, and the signal for the first rush onto the quarterdeck was to be made in the middle of the night when the skipper had the watch. But, as Pelsaert also observed, "God the Lord did not wish to suffer that extraordinary bad evil, but rather let the ship be wrecked." For, in the midst of his plotting and planning, Jacobsz ignored the lookout's warning of breakers ahead, and the *Batavia* sailed onto the rocks at a group of islets off the western Australian coast, roughly abreast of the present city of Geraldton.

"Fourth of June, being Monday morning, on the 2 day of Whitsuntide, with a clear full moon about two hours before daybreak during the watch of the skipper," wrote Pelsaert in his journal, "I was lying in my bunk feeling ill and felt suddenly, with a rough terrible movement, the bumping of the ship's rudder, and immediately after I fell out of my bunk." Gathering himself together, he dashed up to deck, where he found that the sails were full, the wind southwest, and that the ship lay in the middle of a thick spray of breakers. He shouted at Jacobsz, "What have you done? Skipper, what have you done that through your reckless carelessness you have run this noose round our necks?" — at which Jacobsz merely shrugged, saying, "How could I do better?"

Taxed further, the skipper blamed the gunner, saying that when he had seen the breakers in the distance he had asked the gunner what he thought, and had received the reassurance that it was just the shine of the moon on the water. Dismissing this nonsense, Pelsaert then demanded to know where they were, to which Jacobsz said, "God knows." Giving up the argument, the Commandeur ordered the men to sound the water all around the ship, and found that it was less than eighteen feet deep, which was very bad news indeed.

Wrecking was unfortunately rather common with the East Indiamen of any nation (though this was the first on Australia), there being no way of calculating longitude at the time, but the *Batavia* was extraordinarily unlucky. The ship had run ashore at high tide, so there was no way of floating or kedging her off. Abandoning ship was the only option.

But nothing was easy. When a boat was released from its lashings a squall of rain scooted it overboard, and it could not be retrieved until the yawl — a small boat with just four oars — was sent down after it. While that was being done, day dawned, and looking around, Pelsaert realized the full extent of the tragedy — that the ship was high on the rocks, with shallows on every side.

The skipper was sent off in the yawl to look for a landing place, and returned to say he had spied a couple of islands, but had not been able to land because the yawl was too small. Meantime, there total chaos had taken over the ship — what Pelsaert called a "great Yammer." Women wept and children screamed, while their menfolk moaned and wrung their hands, and the soldiers had broken into the spirit room, and were running amok. Accordingly, Pelsaert decided to get the passengers onto some kind of land as fast as possible, while the seamen salvaged what provisions they could from the flooding holds.

"But God the Lord," as he despaired, "chastised us with many rods." The evacuation was very slow, because of the rocks and the cant of the wreck, and so by sunset only about "180 souls, 20 Casks of bread and some small barrels of water" had been landed. And then the skipper returned from the two islands where the passengers had been landed, to report that there was no fresh water on either shore. "What's the point of trying to save water when they all drink as much as they like?" he asked, and advised that the Commandeur should do something about rationing the supplies.

At that, Pelsaert went down in Jacobsz' boat to oversee a search for a better island — and found it impossible to get back to the wreck. Try as he might, the wind and tide were right against him. About seventy men were still perched on the canted hull, including Jeronimus Cornelisz , but nothing could be done about them until the weather moderated. Accordingly, he and the skipper joined about forty castaways on one of the islands — the one that was later called Traitors Island — and made an inventory of what scant provisions were there, coming to the rapid conclusion that their position was hopeless. Frustratingly, back on the ship there was a good store of water that had been taken on at the Cape of Good Hope, but there was no way of getting at it, unless the ship broke up and the barrels floated out unscathed, which was hardly likely to happen.

So, in good Dutch style, they held a committee meeting, and the resolution was made "that we should go in search of water on the islands most nearby or on the continent to keep them and us alive, and if we could find no water, that we should then sail the boat without delay to Batavia, with God's grace there to relate our sad, unheard of, disastrous happening." And so Pelsaert and Jacobsz sailed off, taking the uppersteersman, the understeersmen and the high boatswain with them, along with about forty seamen and passengers, not forgetting Zwaantie Hendrix, Jacobsz' mistress, who had been Lucretia's vindictive maid. Two hundred and sixty eight castaways were left behind. Seventy of them still on the wreck, and all the others were on the other island, which by now had been called Batavia's Graveyard.

Of course those that Pelsaert and the skipper had left behind felt deeply betrayed. As Gijsbert Bastiaensz, the Predikant, said later, they "left us there sad and miserable: having no drink of Wine or Water in four or five days, so that we had to drink our own water, and also many died from thirst." On the sixth day of the marooning, it rained, and then the wind and sea died down, so that those whose survived on the wreck could get to the island by clinging to various pieces of flotsam and jetsam. Cornelisz floated ashore on a mast. And, while the Predikant said that he "in the beginning behaved himself very well," setting the castaways to making rafts so that both provisions and treasure could be salvaged from the wreck, it was then that another nightmare began to unfold.

A council was elected by the castaways, and Cornelisz was elected as chairman, which suited him very well. His secret intention was to escape by going on board any passing ship that responded to their signals of distress, murdering their crew, and taking over their vessel — but, while he found some willing co-conspirators, there were far too many people to co-opt into the plot, and too many witnesses to be left behind. So he embarked on a campaign of assassination.

The process of eliminating unwanted castaways began when two soldiers broke into a wine cask, and were found dead drunk. A meeting of the council was held, the two men were convicted. Then, giving what he thought were logical reasons for his argument, Cornelisz proposed the death penalty. This extreme measure made the council nervous, and when they demurred he took open control, and dismissed them. Then he formed another council — and, according to the Predikant, this time he had the choice of the members, and naturally appointed men from his secret cabal. And so the murders began.

The two drunken soldiers, along with two others, were tied up, taken on a raft to Traitors Island, and drowned. A fifth, Andries de Vries, had also been tied up, but he was spared on the condition that he would do whatever he was ordered, including cutting the throats of those who were lying in the tent that had been set up for the sick. Other deaths were supposed to be brought about without violence, simply by letting the victims die of thirst. Cornelisz ordered some of his men to build rafts, and go out on them to explore another island for water, and when they returned to report failure, he told them to shut up. Then, letting it be falsely known that there was plenty of water on the island — now called Seals Island — he sent a forty-five-strong party to settle there. A few of these managed to eke out an existence, so Cornelisz sent men to kill them. Another party, including the provost and his wife, was marooned on Traitors Island. They, too, managed to survive — until the day that three of Cornelisz' councilors arrived in a small boat. Screaming, the castaways tried to flee, and one by one they were hunted down and slaughtered. There was also treachery — Cornelisz would politely invite a married couple for a meal in his tent, and while they were being entertained, his councilors would murder their children. In these various ways, one hundred and twenty-five castaways were killed.

As the word got around and the murders became more open, panic ruled on Batavia's Graveyard. The only reprieve was perceived as being two and a half miles off, at an islet that had been called High Island. Earlier, as part of Cornelisz' plan to let people die naturally of thirst, he had sent a party of soldiers there. Their leader, a sergeant named Wiebbe Hayes, had been more resourceful than most, and had set his men to digging holes, which proved to yield drinkable water. They had managed to club birds and wallabies, finding them easy prey and good eating. Now, because of the smoke of their fires, it was known that they had survived, and the innocent were desperate to join them. Accordingly, rafts were being hurriedly constructed, while one man succeeded in getting to High Island in a tiny homemade skiff.

Meantime, as Wiebbe Hayes testified later, Lucretia was suffering her own ordeal, as Cornelisz had forcibly taken her into his tent, being determined to make her his concubine. Even after being captured and imprisoned, she fought him determinedly — as Cornelisz said to her later, during his trial, "It is true, you are not to blame for it for you were in my tent for twelve days before I could succeed." In the end, he resorted to grim threats to get her into his bed. According to Cornelisz' own account, he complained to one of his councilors "that he could not accomplish his ends either with kindness or anger." The councilor, David van Seevanck, answered with a laugh, "And don't you know how to manage that? I'll soon make her do it."

Then he went into the tent, and said to Lucretia, "I hear complaints about you."

"On what account?" said she.

"Because you do not comply with the Captain's wishes in kindness; now however, you will have to make up your mind, either you will go the same way as Wybrecht Claes, or else you must do that for which we have kept the women."

Wybrecht Claes, the servant of the Predikant's wife, had been murdered while Cornelisz had been entertaining the Predikant and his pretty eldest daughter, as Lucretia knew well. "Through this threat," said Wiebbe Hayes, "Lucretia had to consent that day and thus he had her as his concubine for the time of two months."

Once he had her, Cornelisz was possessive of her, forbidding all other men to even speak to his lovely concubine. When de Vries, the man who had been ordered to murder the sick people, was seen talking to Lucretia, Cornelisz, in a blind rage, ordered him killed. Terrified, de Vries ran down to the sea and into the water, and there he was brought down by one of the councilors, and knifed to death. It was noon, in the open sun, so the murder was witnessed by many terrified castaways, including Lucretia herself.

Cornelisz and the other rulers of Batavia's Graveyard were also beginning to find the growing army on High Island an irritation. When one of the councilors was sent over with a letter, to try and bribe some of the soldiers onto the mutineers' side, he was kept prisoner. This led to an attack, which Wiebbe Hayes fought off in a decisive action, despite the lack of weapons. Being relatively well fed, his men were able to fight with strength and spirit, and so the councilors' party was defeated. When they returned with the shameful news, Cornelisz, furious at what he saw as their cowardice, decided to lead his own assault. But, much to the delight of the surviving castaways on Batavia's Graveyard, Cornelisz was decisively defeated. Then, after he had been tied up by Hayes and his men, he suffered the indignity of being imprisoned in a pit.

Back on Batavia's Graveyard, however, the general joy was quickly muted. The place of Chairman of the Council was promptly taken over by another brute, Wouter Loos, who also moved into Cornelisz' tent. Whether Loos seized successor's rights and raped Lucretia is one of history's secrets. His ultimate punishment was not hanging, but marooning on the mainland of western Australia (an ordeal from which he never emerged) instead, which indicates that he may have not. He was busy enough, as it happened, as he felt such a strong loyalty to Cornelisz that he immediately organized a rescue mission.

The attack Loos mounted on High Island had unexpected results, because Wiebbe Hayes suddenly vanished from the battle front. Up to that moment, he had been leading his men to the defense with his usual spirit, but then an incoming sail was raised, and he immediately left the battle to his second in command, and leapt into the skiff. Paddling hard, he came up with the vessel — to find it was the same East Indiaman *Sardam* that had sailed from Amsterdam in convoy with the *Batavia*. And that Francisco Pelsaert was on board. Miraculously, the Commandeur had survived the open boat passage to Java.

Pelsaert's boat, with all the *Batavia*'s officers on board, had arrived at Batavia — "God be thanked and praised" — ten weeks earlier, on 7 July The instant the merchant hobbled on shore he had lodged a furious report, with such effect that just three days later the High Boatswain was hanged for his part in the assault on Lucretia. And, three days after that, Jacobsz, who must have been deeply regretting so ill-advisedly coming with Pelsaert, was arrested for negligence in the wrecking of the *Batavia*. Then, with such urgency that he didn't delay to watch the traitor being sentenced and hanged, Pelsaert had boarded the *Sardam*, and sailed pell-mell for the wreck site. Unfortunately, he had been held up by terrible weather, but now at last he was here.

The story Hayes told Pelsaert and the skipper of the *Sardam* appalled them both, though he did have a little enlivening news — that he held the ringleader prisoner. Not long after he had finished his tale, the members of Cornelisz' council arrived at the side of the *Sardam* with a hastily prepared story, but with Hayes there to identify their crimes, they were speedily put in shackles. Next morning, Hayes led the *Sardam*'s boat and yawl to High Island, where they rescued his soldiers and retrieved the bound body of Cornelisz, and from there the two boats headed for Batavia's Graveyard, where the rest of the murderers were arrested.

From then on, it was a grim story of retribution. All the prisoners were put on Traitors Island, as its isolation and barrenness made it as good as a jail, and as the days passed by they were brought one by one to Batavia's Graveyard for examination. This, undoubtedly, involved the threat of torture. Whether freely or forcibly given, the testimony horrified those present.

Eight, including Cornelisz, were condemned to death, a verdict that was followed by a kind of ritual, in which there was a public reading of examinations and sentences. When this grim recitation was finished, Cornelisz spoke up to beg for a reprieve, to give him time to be baptized. This was granted, but instead of sending for the Predikant, he wrote two letters proclaiming his innocence, which he secretly gave to one of the understeersmen. When these were intercepted he was threatened again with torture, at which he confessed to all his crimes.

And so Pelsaert intoned his slightly revised sentence — *Jeronimus Cornelisz, of Haarlem, Apothecary, and late under Merchant of the ship* Batavia, *on Monday, being the first of October, as he has requested to be baptised, to Seals Island, to a place made ready for it in order to exercise Justice, and there first to cut off both his hands, and after shall be punished on the Gallows with the Cord till Death shall follow, with the confiscation of all his money, gold Silver, monthly wages, and all claims which here in India he may have against the profits of the Gen. East India Company, our Lord Masters."*

All eight condemned men were taken to Seal Island, where Cornelisz had once sent men and women to die of thirst, and where now a gibbet had been raised. In a final gesture of contempt, Cornelisz' seven companions all requested that he should be the first to be hanged, so they could watch him dangle.

The *Sardam* finally arrived at Batavia on December 5, 1629, having been delayed by many attempts to salvage treasure from the *Batavia* wreck. Lucretia walked off the ship with her head held high. It was either then or earlier that she found that she was a widow, but she was still rich enough and beautiful enough to attract suitors. In October 1630 she remarried, still in Batavia, where she had remained as a respected figure.

SOURCES

1. The Nantucket Cook: A version of this story was published in *Mains'l Haul*, the journal of the Maritime Museum of San Diego, v. 42, no. 4, Fall 2006. The anecdote originally appeared in *An Old Sailor's Yarns,* by Captain Roland Folger Coffin (Funk & Wagnalls, 1884) and was retold in *The Story of the New England Whalers,* by John r. Spears (NY: Macmillan, 1908) pp. 265-272.

2. Mary Ann Jewell: This story is greatly lengthened and elaborated from an early short version that I wrote for *Mains'l Haul,* as cited above. The details about the cabin built by the *Grafton* castaways come from Joan Druett, *Island of the Lost,* (NY: Algonquin, 2007). Background facts were gleaned from *The General Grant's Gold,* by Madelene Allen and Ken Scadden (Auckland, NZ: Exisle Press, 2007), and *The Wreck of the* General Grant, by Keith Eunson (Wellington, NZ: AH & AW Reed, 1974), while the thrust of the story was taken from the account written by Joseph Jewell to his parents, from Ross, New Zealand, dated July 16, 1868, the original of which is in Te Papa National Museum of New Zealand. Also see the *Southland Times,* January 20,

1868, and the website "Wreck of the General Grant," which has a transcript of the William Sanguilly narrative, as well as the Jewell letter, and briefly sketches what happened to the Jewells after their rescue.

3. Emily Wooldridge: As described, Emily Wooldridge kept a journal of her terrible experience, which was published as *The Wreck of the* Maid of Athens, *Being the Journal of Emily Wooldridge 1869-1870,* edited by Laurence Irving (NY: Macmillan, 1953). Irving's account of how he obtained the manuscript is so bizarre that it's possible to wonder if the journal is a fake. However the ship's registration and the wreck and rescue are all on record, and the sedate tone and matter-of-fact style of the diary is convincing.

4. Encounters with Pirates: Much of this appeared in a story I wrote for *Mains'l Haul,* V. 56, no.4, Fall 2000. As it was rewritten, more anecdotes were added. Mary Brewster's journals were published as *She Was a Sister Sailor: Mary Brewster's Whaling Journals, 1845-1851* (Mystic, CT: Mystic Seaport Museum, 1992), edited and with a commentary by Joan Druett. Dr. John Wilson's journal was published as *The Cruise of the 'Gipsy': The Journal of John Wilson, Surgeon on a Whaling Voyage to the Pacific Ocean 1839-1843.* Edited by Honore Forster (Fairfield, Washington: Ye Galleon Press, 1990). Robert Owen's journal kept on *Warrens* of London is held by the New Bedford Whaling Museum, Kendall Collection. Eliza Underwood's partial journal on the *Kingsdown* is held at the Dixson Library, State Library of New South Wales, Sydney, Australia; also see *Rough Medicine, Surgeons at Sea in the Age of Sail,* by Joan Druett (NY: Routledge, 2001).. A transcript of Nancy Follansbee's journal on the *Logan* 1837-39 is held at the Peabody-Essex Museum in Salem, Massachusetts. Also see *Petticoat*

Whalers (Auckland, NZ: Collins, 1991) by Joan Druett. The story of the *Flying Fox* was told in *Whaling Ways of Hobart Town* by J.E. Philp (Hobart, Tas.: 1936), p.41. Charlotte Babcock's typed reminiscence, titled "Life on the Ocean Wave: Reminiscences of my Voyages Around the World, 1851-8" is held at the Huntington Library in San Marino, California. For the "Horrible Massacre of a Crew of A South Sea Whaler" see the New Bedford *Whalemen's Shipping List,* January 1, 1861.

5.The *Living Age*: A very short version of this was within the article I published in the Fall 2000 issue of *Mains'l Haul* cited above. My source at the time was Suzanne J. Stark's fine story, "Mates at Sea: The Adventures of 19th Century Captains' Wives," in *Seaport* XX no. 1 (Spring 1986): 29. Since then, because of the kindness of Rick Spilman, I had access to second mate Hinckley's rousing version, published as *Wrecked on a Reef in the China Sea* in Boston by Fish Printing Co. in 1898. The text of a 1919 interview with Hinckley can be found online in "Medford Historical Society Papers, volume 22." A more formal accounting, based on the report of the consul and the evidence given to the insurance company, can be read in the *Bulletin of the Business Historical Society,* v.11, no. 2 (April 1937), pp. 23-27. Unfortunately, I still don't know Mrs. Holmes' Christian name.

6. Mary Ellen Clarke: Again, I wrote a very short version of the mutiny on the *Frank N. Thayer* for *Mains'l Haul* (Fall 2000). My reference at the time was "Mutiny on the *Thayer*," by Edith Derby Robinson, published in *Long Island Forum* in May 1941, pp. 107-108. The background for this greatly lengthened retelling came from newspapers: "Mutiny and Murder on the High Seas," *News of the World,* February 7, 1886; the Hobart, Tasmania, *Mercury,* March 26, 1886;

and a much later retelling by Asa Bordages, in the New York *World Telegram,* May 18, 1934. Mary Ellen Clarke's obituary in the *Brooklyn Daily Eagle,* August 10, 1909, corrects a lot of journalistic errors. I thank Rick Spilman for this last.

7. Joanna Durie: *Wreck of the Isabella* by David Miller (Annapolis, Maryland: Naval Institute Press, 1995) is a well-researched and thoroughly entertaining account of the wreck and its aftermath, and provides excellent background to the setting, the ships, and the major characters. I also used Joseph Holt's *Memoirs of Joseph Holt,* edited by Thomas Crofton Croker, and published in London in 1838, which is readily available on the internet. Caution had to be taken, as the memoir was not just semi-literate, but also very self-serving, Holt being a very vain, touchy character who insisted on portraying himself as the great hero. Additionally, the editor took great liberties with the manuscript, to make Holt seemed better educated and more genteel (and perhaps a lot more pious) than he actually was. There is a more accurate version of Holt's memoir, *A Rum Story,* edited by Peter O'Shaughnessy (Australia: Kangaroo Press, 1988), but unfortunately it covers only his thirteen years in New South Wales. Also see the entry in *Australian Dictionary of Biography.* Charles H. Barnard published an account of the wreck and his ordeal after marooning in 1836, as *A Narrative of the Sufferings and Adventures....* This has been edited and published with a commentary by Bertha S. Dodge, as *Marooned, being a Narrative of the Sufferings and Adventures* ...(New York: Syracuse University Press, 1986). I used the original version.

8. Rose de Freycinet: I have written about Rose de Freycinet before, she being one of the two major figures in chapter 17 of *She Captains* (NY: Simon & Schuster, 2000). My major source for the voyaging of this winsome young woman is her own letters, translated and edited by Marc Serge Rivière, and beautifully published as *A Woman of Courage* (Canberra: National Library of Australia, 1996). Also see, Marnie Bassett, *Realms and Islands: the World Voyage of Rose de Freycinet..* (London: Oxford University Press, 1962), and John Dunmore, *French Explorers in the Pacific* (Oxford: Clarendon, 1969).

9. Millie Jenkins: This story was taken from the newspaper reports, as cited in the text. There is a file on the loss of the *Kathleen* in the New Bedford Free Public Library, as there also is in the library of the New Bedford Whaling Museum.

10. Gertrude West: The story of Gertrude West and her dream is told in *Whaling Wives,* by Emma Whiting and Henry Beetle Hough (Boston: Houghton Mifflin, 1953). There is also a long article about Gertrude and the wreck in the *San Francisco Call,* 21 May 1899, while the *Western Argus*, of Kalgoolie, Western Australia, ran the story about the strange castaway who remained on the island on 21 February, 1922. There is also a story about the hurricane and the wreck of the *Horatio* in the *Taranaki Herald,* New Zealand, 22 June 1899.

11. Frances Wordsworth: The major source for the story of Mrs. Wordsworth is *Survival on the Crozet Islands,* by Ian Church (Waikanai, NZ: The Heritage Press, 1995). I thank Ian Church for his lively interest and help over the years, and also the library staff of the New Bedford Whaling Museum for background to the voyage of the *Young Phoenix.*

12. Nancy Hopewell: Retold from a story published *The Brooklyn Times,* October 3, 1904. The illustrations come from this, as well.

13. The Anonymous Heroine. As described in the text, the recapture of the brig by the mate's wife was featured in many newspapers, including the *New York Times,* March 1, 1863, where I first read it. They all tell the same story. The colorful history of Vernon Guyon Locke and the steam tug *Uncle Ben* came from *In Armageddon's Shadow: the Civil War and Canada's Maritime Provinces,* by Greg Marquis (Halifax, NS: Gorsebrook Research Institute, 1998). Nichols' report can be found on the website "Civil War Talk," in the section "Military Service Records."

14. Lucretia Jansz. The major source for this was *Voyage to Disaster,* Henrietta Drake-Brockman's classic collection of translated documents, including Pelsaert's journal. (Australia: Angus & Robertson, 1963, republished by the University of Western Australia Press, 1995). There is also a good summary on the website of the Museum of Western Australia, *"Batavia's* History," well illustrated with Dutch woodcuts.

Old Salt Press is an independent press catering to those who love good books about ships and the sea. We are an association of writers working together to produce the very best of nautical and maritime fiction and non-fiction. We invite you to join us as we go down to the sea in books.

New Releases from Old Salt Press

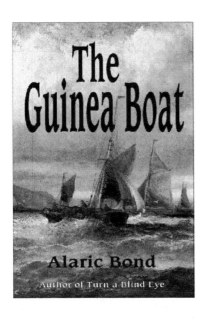

THE GUINEA BOAT

by Alaric Bond

The Guinea Boat is set in Hastings, Sussex during the early part of 1803. Britain is still at an uneasy peace with France, but there is action and intrigue a plenty along the south-east coast. Private fights and family feuds abound; a hot press threatens the livelihoods of many, while the newly re-formed Sea Fencibles begin a careful watch on Bonaparte's ever growing invasion fleet. And to top it all, free trading has grown to the extent that it is now a major industry, and one barely kept in check by the efforts of the preventive men.

ISBN: 978-0-9941152-9-4

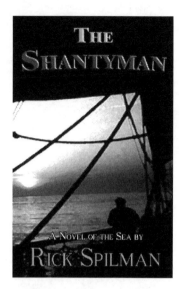

THE SHANTYMAN

by Rick Spilman

In 1870, on the clipper ship *Alahambra* in Sydney, the new crew comes aboard more or less sober, except for the last man, who is hoisted aboard in a cargo sling, paralytic drunk. On a ship with a dying captain and a murderous mate, Barlow will literally keep the crew pulling together. As he struggles with a tragic past, a troubled present and an uncertain future, Barlow's one goal is bringing the ship and crew safely back to New York, where he hopes to start anew.

Based on a true story, The Shantyman is a gripping tale of survival against all odds at sea and ashore, and the challenge of facing a past that can never be wholly left behind.

ISBN: 978-0-9941152-2-5

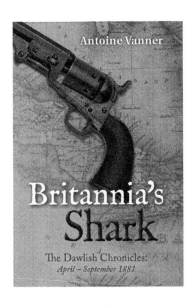

BRITANNIA'S SHARK

by Antoine Vanner

The year is 1881, and a daring act of piracy draws ambitious British navy officer, Nicholas Dawlish, into a deadly maelstrom of intrigue and revolution. In a headlong adventure, Dawlish and his beloved wife, Florence, voyage from the excesses of America's Gilded Age to the fevered squalor of an island ruled by savage tyranny. Manipulated ruthlessly from London by the shadowy Admiral Topcliffe, Nicholas and Florence must make strange alliances if they are to survive — and prevail.

ISBN978-09922636-9-0

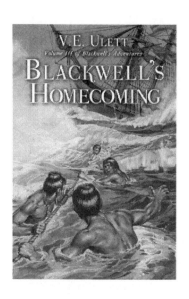

BLACKWELL'S HOMECOMING
by V.E. Ulett

In a multigenerational saga of love, war and betrayal, Captain Blackwell and Mercedes continue their voyage in Volume III of Blackwell's Adventures. The Blackwell family's eventful journey from England to Hawaii, by way of the new and tempestuous nations of Brazil and Chile, provides an intimate portrait of family conflicts and loyalties in the late Georgian Age. *Blackwell's Homecoming* is an evocation of the dangers and rewards of desire.

ISBN 978-09882360-7-3

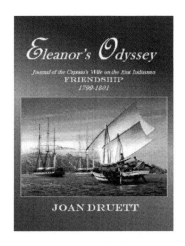

ELEANOR'S ODYSSEY by Joan Druett

"In 1799, the twenty-one-year-old Eleanor Reid accepted her new husband's invitation to accompany him on a voyage from Ireland to Australia and back to England — via St. Helena, Cape Town, Sydney, Malacca, and Calcutta. She was a keen observer of the natural and social worlds, and her riveting memoir brims with insights at once worldly and intimate. I can imagine no abler guide to the remote yet cosmopolitan world through which Reid sailed than Joan Druett, whose introductory narratives provide the historical context *Eleanor's Odyssey* so richly deserves."

— Lincoln Paine, award-winning author of *The Sea and Civilization*

"This book is two joys in one. Eleanor's tale is told so compellingly that it could be mistaken for a novel - although it isn't. Full of wise insights, it is an important addition to the study of sea history."

– Jo Stanley, leading expert on women and the sea, and author of *Bold In Her Breeches*.

ISBN 978-0-9941152-1-8

Also proudly produced by Old Salt Press

HELL AROUND THE HORN by Rick Spilman. A nautical thriller set in the last days of sail. ISBN: 978-09882360-1-1

TURN A BLIND EYE by Alaric Bond. England is at war with Napoleon, but smuggling is rife on the south coast of England. ISBN: 978-09882360-3-5

TORRID ZONE by Alaric Bond. She's a tired ship with a worn-out crew, yet HMS *Scylla* must venture again into enemy-ridden seas. The sixth in the Fighting Sail series. ISBN: 978-09882360-9-7

CAPTAIN BLACKWELL'S PRIZE by V.E. Ulett. A romantic adventure from the days of wooden ships and iron men. ISBN: 978-09882360-6-6

CAPTAIN BLACKWELL'S PARADISE by V.E. Ulett. Book number two in the rousing Blackwell series. ISBN: 978-09882360-5-9

THE ELEPHANT VOYAGE by Joan Druett. The rescue of six castaways in the sub-Antarctic leads to international controversy. ISBN: 978-09922588-4-9

THE BECKONING ICE by Joan Druett. Wiki Coffin battles a vicious murderer in the icy sub-Antarctic. The fifth in the Wiki Coffin historical maritime murder mystery series. ISBN: 978-09922588-3-2

Joan Druett, a proud founding member of Old Salt Press, is a maritime historian and an expert on whaling history and women at sea, and also the author of the bestseller *Island of the Lost*. Her books have received many awards, including the John Lyman Award for Best Book of American Maritime History, the L. Byrne Waterman Award, and a New York Public Library Best Book to Remember Award. Her scholarships include a Fulbright Fellowship and a Stout Fellowship. She lives in New Zealand with her husband, the internationally acclaimed maritime artist, Ron Druett, who contributed much of the artwork for this book.

Made in the USA
Middletown, DE
07 September 2016